WITHDRAWN

CHESHIRE

A GENEALOGICAL BIBLIOGRAPHY

Volume 2

Cheshire Family Histories
and
Pedigrees

by

Stuart A. Raymond

Published by the
Federation of Family History Societies (Publications) Ltd,
The Benson Room, Birmingham & Midland Institute,
Margaret Street, Birmingham , B3 3BS, England

Copies also obtainable from:

S.A. & M.J. Raymond, 6, Russet Avenue, Exeter, EX1 3QB, U.K.

First Published 1995

Cataloguing in publication data:

Raymond, Stuart A., 1945-
Cheshire: a genealogical bibliography. 2 vols British genealogical
bibliographies. Birmingham, England: Federation of Family History
Societies, 1995. Vol. 1. Cheshire genealogical sources. Vol. 2. Cheshire
family histories and pedigrees.

DDC 016.9291094271

ISBN 1-86006-012-9

ISSN 1033-2065

CONTENTS

VOLUME 2: Cheshire Family Histories and Pedigrees

VOLUME 1: Cheshire Genealogical Sources

Introduction

This bibliography is intended primarily for genealogists. It is, however, hoped that it will also prove useful to historians, librarians, archivists, research students, and anyone else interested in the history of Cheshire. It is intended to be used in conjunction with my *English genealogy: an introductory bibliography,* and the other volumes in the *British genealogical bibliographies* series. A full list of these volumes appears on the back cover. The area covered is the historic county of Cheshire, as it existed prior to local government reorganisation in 1974.

Published sources of information on Cheshire genealogy are listed in volume 1 of the present work; this volume lists works devoted to specific families, together with collections of pedigrees, biographical dictionaries, and heraldry. It includes published books and journal articles, but excludes the numerous notes and queries found in family history society and similar journals, except where the content is of importance. Where I have included such notes, replies to them are cited in the form 'see also', with no reference to the names of respondents. This is a bibliography of published works; hence the many manuscript family histories and pedigrees to be found in Cheshire libraries are excluded. Where possible, citations are accompanied by notes indicating the period covered, locality/ies in which particular families dwelt, and other pertinent information.

Anyone who tries to compile a totally comprehensive bibliography of Cheshire is likely to fall short of his aim. The task is almost impossible, especially if the endeavour is made by one person. That does not, however, mean that the attempt should not be made. Usefulness, rather than comprehensiveness, has been my prime aim - and this book will not be useful to anyone if its publication were to be prevented by a vain attempt to ensure total comprehensiveness. I am well aware that there are likely to be omissions - although none, I hope, of books which every Cheshire genealogist should examine. My purpose has been to enable you to identify works which are mostly readily available, and which can be borrowed via the inter-library loan network irrespective of whether you live in London or Melbourne. Most public libraries are able to tap into this network; your local library should be able to borrow most items I have listed, even if it has to go overseas to obtain them.

If you are an assiduous researcher, you may well come across items I have missed. If you do, please let me know, so that they can be included in the next edition.

The work of compiling this bibliography has depended heavily on the resources of the libraries I have used. These included Cheshire Record Office, Stockport Local Heritage Library, Chester City Record Office, Chester Public Library, Manchester Public Library, Exeter University Library, Exeter City Library, the British Library, and the Society of Genealogists, amongst others. I am grateful to the librarians of all these institutions for their help. I am grateful too for the assistance rendered by the three family history societies in Cheshire, and particularly to Peter Dewdney and Brenda Smith. Brian Christmas and Brett Langston both kindly read and commented on early drafts of the book, Jean Smith typed the manuscript, and Bob Boyd saw the book through the press. I am grateful too to the officers of the Federation of Family History Societies, whose support is vital for the continuation of this series. My thanks also to my wife Marjorie, and to Paul and Mary, who have lived with this book for many months.

Stuart A. Raymond

Libraries and Record Offices

Chester Library,
Northgate Street,
CHESTER,
Cheshire,
CH1 2EF

Stockport Local Heritage Library,
Stockport Central Library,
Wellington Road South,
STOCKPORT,
SK1 3RS

Cheshire Record Office,
Duke Street,
Chester,
Cheshire,
CH1 1RL

Chester City Record Office,
Town Hall,
Chester,
Cheshire,
CH1 2HJ

John Rylands University Library of Manchester,
Oxford Road,
Manchester,
M13 9PP

In addition, most public libraries have local collections relating to their own localities. For full details, see the *Directory of local studies in North West England,* cited in volume 1, section 2.

Abbreviations

A.N.Q.	*Advertiser notes and queries*
C.F.H.	*Cheshire family historian*
C.N.Q.	*Cheshire notes and queries*
C.P.R.M.	*Cheshire parish registers: marriages*
C.Sf.	*Cheshire sheaf*
Cm.S.	Chetham Society
F.H.S.C.	Family History Society of Cheshire
F.H.S.C.J.	*Family History Society of Cheshire Journal*
H.S.L.C.	*Transactions of the Historic Society of Lancashire and Cheshire*
J.C.A.H.S.	*Journal of the Chester Archaeological and Historic Society*
J.L.D.L.H.S.	*Journal of the Lymm and District Local History Society*
L.C.A.S.	*Transactions of the Lancashire and Cheshire Antiquarian Society*
L.C.R.S.	Lancashire and Cheshire Record Society
L.G.	*Local Gleanings*
M.G.H.	*Miscellanea genealogica et heraldica*
N.C.F.H.	*North Cheshire family historian*
N.C.F.H.S.	North Cheshire Family History Society
N.S.	New series
O.S.	Old series
P.N.	*Palatine note-book*
P.P.R.S.	Phillimore's parish register series
Q.J.L.D.	*Quarterly journal of the Lymm and District Local History Society*

Bibliographic Presentation

Authors' names are in SMALL CAPITALS. Book and journal titles are in *italics*. Articles appearing in journals, and material such as parish register transcripts, forming only part of books are in inverted commas and textface type. Volume numbers are in **bold** and the individual number of the journal may be shown in parentheses. These are normally followed by the place of publication (except where this is London, which is omitted), the name of the publisher and the date of publication. In the case of articles, further figures indicate page numbers.

1. PEDIGREE COLLECTIONS AND BIOGRAPHICAL DICTIONARIES, etc.

The modern genealogist stands on the shoulders of his predecessors, amongst whom were the heralds of the sixteenth and seventeenth centuries. They regularly conducted 'visitations' of the counties in order to determine the right of gentry to bear arms. In so doing, they compiled many pedigrees of county families. Many of their collections have been published (although sometimes in corrupt form.) For Cheshire, see:

LANGTON, WILLIAM. ed. *The visitation of Lancashire and a part of Cheshire, made in the twenty-fourth year of the reign of King Henry the Eighth, A.D. 1533, by special commission of Thomas Benalt, Clarencieux.* Cm.S., O.S., 98 & 110. 1876-82.

RYLANDS, JOHN PAUL, ed. *The visitation of Cheshire in the year 1580, made by Robert Glover, Somerset Herald, for William Flower, Norroy King of Arms, with numerous additions and continuations, including those from the visitation of Cheshire made in the year 1566, by the same herald, with an appendix containing the visitation of a part of Cheshire in the year 1533, made by William Fellows, Lancaster Herald, for Thomas Benolte, Clarenceux King of Arms, and a fragment of the visitation of the City of Chester in the year 1591, made by Thomas Chalenor, deputy to the Office of Arms.* Publications of the Harleian Society 18. 1882.

ARMYTAGE, SIR GEORGE J., & RYLANDS, J. PAUL, eds. *Pedigrees made at the visitation of Cheshire, 1613, taken by Richard St. George, esq., Norroy King of Arms, and Henry St. George, gent., Bluemantle Pursuivant of Arms, and some other contemporary pedigrees.* Publications of the Harleian Society 59. 1909. Also published as L.C.R.S. 58. 1909.

RYLANDS, J. PAUL. 'Disclaimers at the Heralds visitations,' *H.S.L.C.* 43-4; N.S., 7-8, 1891-2, 63-90. Mainly in Cheshire 1613-64; also Lancashire, 1667.

ADAMS, A. *Cheshire visitation pedigrees, 1663.* Publications of the Harleian Society 93. 1941.

I[RVINE], W.F. 'List of pedigrees in Dugdale's visitation of Cheshire, 1663-4', *C.Sf.* 3rd series 36, 1948, 61-7, *passim.*

A collection of pedigrees in the British Library's Harleian manuscripts is indexed in:

PRICE, THOMAS. 'Cheshire pedigrees', *H.S.L.C.* 75; N.S., 39, 21737.

A number of works deal with old Cheshire families and their seats; these should be consulted if you think you are connected to the 'gentry'. See:

ANGUS-BUTTERWORTH, LIONEL MILNER. *Old Cheshire families and their seats.* Manchester: Sherrat and Hughes, 1932. Reprinted Manchester: E.J.Morten, 1970. Includes chapters on the families of Brereton, Carrington, Davenport, Grosvenor, Legh, Leycester, Massey and Booth, Moreton, and Stanley.

CROSTON, JAMES. *The county families of Lancashire and Cheshire.* Manchester: John Heywood, 1887. The families considered are: Stanley, Egerton, Trafford, Warburton, Harrington, Hulton, Grosvenor, Mosley, Mainwaring, Hesketh, and Davenport.

FIGUEIREDO, PETER DE, & TREUHERZ, JULIAN. *Cheshire country houses.* Chichester: Phillimore, 1988. Includes a gazetteer and notes on owners.

ORMEROD, GEORGE. *Miscellanea Palatina: consisting of genealogical essays illustrative of Cheshire and Lancashire families, and of a memoir of the Cheshire Domesday roll.* T. Richards, 1851. Includes notes, pedigrees, etc., regarding the families of Norres, Aldford, Arderne, Banastre, Bredbury, Done, Fitzroger, Gernet, Lathom, Montalt, Orreby, Stanley and Stokeport. Mainly medieval.

ROBINSON, JOHN MARTIN. *A guide to the country houses of the North West.* Constable, 1991. Comprehensive listing; includes brief notes on owners; covers Cheshire, Lancashire, Cumberland and Westmorland.

Biographical dictionaries provide brief accounts of the persons listed. For a list of Cheshire men in Thompson Cooper's *New biographical dictionary*, see:

DREDGE, JOHN INGLE. 'Notable persons connected with Lancashire and Cheshire', *P.N.* 2 1882. 195-6.

For lists of the Cheshire gentry, see:
'Gentlemen of Cheshire knighted by the Earl of Hartford at Leith in Scotland, 1544', *L.G.,* 1879-80, 28-30. List.
S., F. 'Gentry of Cheshire in 1673', *C.Sf.* 3rd series **5**, 1904, 30-31 & 34-5. List from Richard Blome's *Britannia.*
S[TEWART]-B[ROWN], R. 'Cheshire gentry and their houses in 1787', *C.Sf.* 3rd series **10**, 1916, 69-70, 73 & 75. List from Tunnicliffe's *Topographical survey ...*
Brief biographies of historical figures are given in:
SIMPSON, F. 'A few Cheshire worthies', *J.C.A.H.S.* **28**(1), 1928, 106-36.
A number of contemporary biographical dictionaries were published in the late 19th and early 20th centuries. These included:
Cheshire leaders, social and political. Exeter: William Pollard & Co., 1896.
GASKELL, ERNEST. *Cheshire leaders, social and political.* Queenhithe Printing, [190-?]
HEAD, ROBERT. *Cheshire at the opening of the twentieth century.* Pike's new-century series, **11**. Brighton: W.T. Pike & Co., 1904. Includes *Contemporary biographies,* ed. W.T.Pike. The biographical portion of this has been reprinted as:
PIKE, W.T., ed. *A dictionary of Edwardian biography: Cheshire.* Edinburgh: Peter Bell, 1987.
PIKE, W.T., ed. *Liverpool and Birkenhead in the twentieth century: contemporary biographies.* Brighton: W.T. Pike & Co., 1911.
Who's who in Cheshire. Worcester: Ebenezer Baylis & Son, 1935.

2. HERALDRY

A. *General*

A number of grants of arms and funeral certificates are available in print, and are listed here. For heraldry in churches, reference should be made to volume 1, section 6. For a list of heraldic arms in print in various county histories, *etc.,* see:
S., A.G. 'Arms and inscriptions in Cheshire churches and houses', *C.Sf.* 3rd series **33**, 1939, 93-118, *passim.*
General works include:
RYLANDS, W.H. 'Some Lancashire and Cheshire heraldic documents', *H.S.L.C.* **63**; N.S., **27**, 1912, 178-219. Heraldic notes on many families.
TIMMIS-SMITH, P. *Family names and arms of the county of Chester.* Congleton: The editor [1977]. Armorial.
GRIFFIN, RALPH. 'Cheshire arms, c.1490', *M.G.H.* 5th series **8**, 1932-4, 197-201. Arms of Cheshire gentry.
'A Chester ordinary of arms, 1629', *C.Sf.* 3rd series **2**, 1898, *passim.*

B. *Grants of Arms etc.*
Barker
'Barker', *M.G.H.* **1**, 1868, 279. Grant of arms, 1638.

Booth
RYLANDS, W. HARRY. 'Exemplification and confirmation of the Booth arms and quarterings, by Robert Cooke, esquire, Clarenceaux King of Arms, to William Booth, esquire, of London, 1st April 1580, 21st Elizabeth', *H.S.L.C.* **58**; N.S., **22**, 1906, 105-8.

Brereton
MONTAGUE-SMITH, PATRICK W. 'The quarterings of Brereton of Brereton, Cheshire', *Coat of arms* **8**, 1964-5, 281-8. See also **9**, 1966-7, 38. Includes medieval pedigrees.
R[YLANDS,], J.P. 'A curious quartering in the arms of Brereton', *C.Sf.* 3rd series **11**, 1915, 14-15.

Cholmondley
RYLANDS, W.H. 'Some Cheshire heraldic documents', *H.S.L.C.* **60**; N.S., **24**, 1908, 160-

70. Concerns Sir Hugh Cholmeley, 1547, Sir Thomas Venables, 1560, Sir Piers Legh, 1575 and Robert Cholmondley, 1661.
See also Cholmeley

Cunliffe
'Grant of crest by Stephen Martin Leake, Garter, and William Oldys, Norroy to Sir Ellis Cunliffe, Knt., and Baronet, 1760', *M.G.H.* **2**, 1876, 251.

Danson
'Grant of arms to Francis Chatillon Danson of Grasmere, Westmorland, and Birkenhead, Co. Chester, 4 December, 1913', *M.G.H.* 5th series **4**, 1922, 191.

Davenport
'Grant of the arms of Davenport to Rear-Admiral Sir Salusbury Davenport (formerly Pryce Humphreys), C.B., K.C.M., P.C., &c., and Dame Maria his wife, 17 May 1838', *Genealogist* **6**, 1882, 34-5.

Davenport-Handley
'Grant and exemplification of arms to John William Handley Davenport-Handley, of Clipsham Hall, Co. Rutland (formerly John William Handley Davenport of Bramhall Hall, Co. Chester), 7th May 1881', *Genealogist* **7**, 1883, 23.

Egerton
'The Egerton arms', *P.N.* **3**, 1883, 237-8.
'Examples of armorial book-plates', *M.G.H.* **1**, 1868, 299. Includes book-plate of John Egerton of Egerton.

Flower
'Grant of a crest by William Flower of Shareston, dated 25th November, 1571', *M.G.H.* **1**, 1868, 1-2.

Greenall
'Grants of arms', *Genealogist.* **4**, 1880, 286-90. Includes grant to Gilbert Greenall of Runcorn, 1876.

Grosvenor
See Scrope

Hulse
R[YLANDS], J.P. 'Grant of arms by John Domville of Mobberley to Thomas de Hulse, A.D. 1393', *C.Sf.* 3rd Series **8**, 1911, 89. Private grant.

Hulton
RYLANDS, J. PAUL. 'Impressions of armorial seals of Cheshire gentry, made by Elias Ashmole in 1663', *H.S.L.C.* **71**, N.S., **35**, 1919, 58-82. Includes pedigrees of Hulton of Chester Pownall of Barnton, Streete of Chester and Taylour of Chester, 17th c..

Ince
B[ENNETT], J.H.E. 'Arms in Alderman Ince's house in Chester', *C.Sf.* 3rd series **13**, 1918, 84-5. See also 96.

Legh
See Cholmeley

Leigh-Mallory
'The Leigh-Mallory patents of arms', *Genealogist* N.S., **32**, 1916, 116-20. 1833.

Leycester
HEWITT, JOHN. 'Arms of Leycester of Toft', *C.Sf.* 3rd series **9**, 1913, 63-4 & 67.

Ling
'Grants of arms', *Genealogist* **5**, 1881, 142-6. Includes 19th c. grants to Ling of Northenden.

Macclesfield
MAXFIELD, DAVID K. 'The supposed arms of Jordan de Macclesfield', *Cheshire history* **32**, 1993, 29-32.

Nunn
'Grant of arms to Rev. Samuel Nunn, 1885', *M.G.H.* 2nd series **2**, 1888, 88.

Pownall
See Hulton

Ridgway
RYLANDS, J. PAUL. 'Examples of amorial bookplates: Ridgway', *M.G.H.* 3rd series **3**, 1880, 47. Of Cheshire and Lancashire; genealogical notes, 19th c.

Rowe
'Grant of a crest to Samuel Rowe of Macclesfield, esq., 1653', *L.G.* 1(11), 1880, 477-9.

Scrope
STEWART-BROWN, R. 'The Scrope and Grosvenor controversy', *H.S.L.C.* **89**, 1937, 1-22. Discussion of case in the Court of Chivalry, concerning the right of Grosvenor to bear arms, 14th c. Includes extensive list of witnesses on behalf of Grosvenor.

Smethwick
'Confirmation of arms to William Smethwick of Smethwick, Co. Chester, 1579', *M.G.H.* 2nd series **1**, 1886, 324.

Streete
See Hulton

Swetenham
'Grant of a crest to Lawrence Swetenham of Somerford Bouths, Co. Chester', *L.G.* 1(7), 1880, 267-70. 1568.

Taylour
See Hulton

Venables
See Cholmeley

Watson
'Grant of arms to William Watson of Lancelyn in the parish of Bebington, Co. Chester, and the other descendants of his father, 1905', *M.G.H.* 5th series **4**, 1920-22, 155.

Wilbraham
R[YLANDS], J.P. 'Quarterings of the Wilbraham family', *C.Sf.* 3rd series **9**, 1913, 105.

Yardley
HEWITT, JOHN. 'Yardley family', *C.Sf.* 3rd series **14**, 1919, 70-71. Arms.

C. *Funeral Certificates.*
For a comprehensive edition of funeral certificates drawn up by the Heralds, see:
RYLANDS, J. PAUL, ed. *Cheshire and Lancashire funeral certificates, A.D. 1600 to 1678.* L.C.R.S. **6**. 1882.

See also:
'Funeral certificates', *Genealogist* **7**, 1883, 112-5 & 142-4; N.S., **1**, 1884, 184-6; **2**, 1885, 85-7.

Aldersey
'The funeral of William Aldersey of Chester, 1615', *C.Sf.* 3rd series **46**, 1952, 4-5 & 8-9. Funeral certificate.

Allen
See Fletcher

Aston
'Funeral certificates', *M.G.H.* **1**, 1868, 85-8. Of the Aston, Norres and Glascoe families, 1606.

Bestone
See Massey

Brereton
See Massey

Brerwood
See Massey

Bretterghe
See Massey

Brooke
RYLANDS, J.P. 'Funeral of Lady Brooke of Norton, 1650', *C.Sf.* **2** 1883, 244-5. Funeral certificate.

Broughton
See Fletcher

Bunbury
See Massey

Cholmondeleigh
See Massey

Domville
THOMAS, G.H. 'The funeral certificate of Edward Domville, esq., 1639', *Q.J.L.D.* **5**(3), 1982, 4-5. Of Lymm.

Dore
See Massey

Dukenfield
See Fletcher

Dymock
See Shakerley

Egerton
'Ralph Egerton of Ridley', *C.Sf.* **2**, 1883, 284-5. Funeral certificate, 1619.

Fletcher
'Funeral certificates', *M.G.H.* **1**, 1868, 43-6. Of the Fletcher, Leigh, Broughton, Martyn *alias* Dukenfield, Allen and Gerrard families, 1598-1601.

Gamul
HUGHES, T. 'The Gamuls of Chester and Buerton', *C.Sf.* **3**, 1891, 89-90. Includes funeral certificate of William Gamul, 1643.

Gerrard
See Fletcher

Glascoe
See Aston

Green
See Massey

Grosvenor
HUGHES, T. 'Richard Grosvenor of Eaton, esquire', *C.Sf.* **2**, 1883, 331-2. Funeral certificate, 1619.
HUGHES, T. 'The funeral of Sir Richard Grosvenor, Bart', *C.Sf.* **2**, 1883, 354-5. Funeral certificate, 1664.

Holford
See Massey

Leech
See Massey

Leigh
See Fletcher

Legh
See Massey

Mainwaring
HUGHES, T. 'Sir Randle Mainwaring, Knight', *C.Sf.* **3**, 1891, 66. Funeral certificate, 1612.

Martyn
See Fletcher

Massey
'Funeral certificates: Cheshire, Lancashire, Shropshire and North Wales', *M.G.H.* **1**, 1868, 27-35. Relating to Massey, Dore, Bunbury, Green, Bretterghe, Cholmondeleigh, Poole, Legh, Leech, Bestone and Sutton families, 1601.

Norres
See Aston

Poole
See Massey

Shakerley
'Funeral certificates, 17th century', *C.Sf.* **2**, 1883, 216-7. Of Jeffery Shakerley, 1619, and William Dymond of Willington, Flintshire, 1620.

Stafford
'Funeral certificates', *M.G.H.* 5th series **8**, 1932-4, 50. Includes certificate of Barbara Stafford nee Twysden of Chester, 1630.

Sutton
See Massey

Thropp
RYLANDS, J.P. 'Chester funeral processions', *C.Sf.* **2**, 1883, 268-9. Funeral certificate of Elianor Thropp, 1639.

Twysden
See Stafford

Wilbraham
HUGHES, T. 'Wilbrahams of Woodhey', *C.Sf.* **3**, 1891, 35-6. See also 57. Funeral certificate of Thomas Wilbraham, 1610.

3. FAMILY HISTORIES, etc.

A considerable amount of research on Cheshire families has been published. This listing includes books and journal articles; it does not, however, include the many brief queries published in family history society and similar journals, except where substantial information is provided. Where such queries are listed, replies to them are cited by page numbers *etc.*, without reference to the name(s) of the respondent(s). Studies which have not been published are not listed. Many pedigrees of particular families are listed here; for collections of pedigrees, see section 1.

Adams

AXON, GEOFFREY R. 'Roger and Orion Adams, printers', *L.C.A.S.* **39**, 1921, 108-24. 18th c.

GLEAVE, GEORGE. 'The Adams family of Woodchurch', *C.Sf.* 3rd series **2**, 1898, 48-9. 17th c.

HUGHES, T. 'Early emigrants to America: the Adams family of Chester', *C.Sf.* **3**, 1891, 139-40. 17-18th c.

Adshead

MYERS, PRUE WALLIS, & KENDRICK, MYRA. 'The Adshead family and Bowdon', *The Bowdon sheaf* **23**, 1994, 5-8. 20th c.

Alcock

DALE, ALAN. 'Alcock', *Lancashire and Cheshire historian* **2**, 1966, 305-6. Quaker entries in Mobberley parish register, 17-18th c.

Aldersey

BRIDGEMAN, C.G.O. *A genealogical account of the family of Aldersey, of Aldersey and Spurstow, Co. Chester.* Chiswick Press, 1899. Includes extensive deed abstracts, 13-19th c., also folded pedigrees.

'Mr. William Aldersey's collections of the mayors of Chester, &c., with notes on the Aldersey family', *C.Sf.* N.S., **1**, 1895, 120-22, 123-4 & 126-8. See also 156-7. 16-17th c., includes will of Raufe Aldersey, 1555.

Allen

RYLANDS, J.PAUL. 'A pedigree of the family of Allen, of Chester and of Brindley, Co. Chester', *Genealogist* N.S., **34**, 1918, 147-8. 16-17th c.

'The Allen bible and family entries', *Cheshire genealogist* **12**, 1993, 20. Entries in Allen family bible, 18-20th c.

Andrews

THELWALL, R.E. *The Andrews and Compstall, their village.* [Chester]: Cheshire County Council Libraries and Museums/Marple Antiquarian Society, 1972. 18-19th c., includes pedigrees, also pedigree of Prescot, 18-19th c..

Antrobus

ANTROBUS, SIR REGINALD L. *Antrobus pedigrees: the story of a Cheshire family.* Mitchell Hughes and Clarke, 1929. 15-20th c.

ANTROBUS, R.H. *Pedigree of Antrobus extracted from the records of the Heralds' College, London.* Congleton: B.Hood, 1969. 17-18th c.

Arderne

See Done

Ashley

'Gems from the 1891 census: the Ashleys of Frodsham', *Frodsham and District Local History Group journal* **16**, 1993, 6.

Aston

LITTLEDALE, WILLOUGHBY ASTON. 'Bible entries: Aston of Aston, Co. Chester', *M.G.H.* 4th series **2**, 1908, 210-12. 17-18th c.

Audeley

BEAMONT, WILLIAM, ed. *Tracts written in the controversy respecting the legitimacy of Amicia, daughter of Hugh Cyveliok, Earl of Chester, AD 1673-1679, by Sir Peter Leycester, Bart., and Sir Thomas Mainwaring, Bart., reprinted from the collection at Peover.* Cm.S., O.S. **78-80.** 1869. Includes pedigrees of Audeley and Nevile, medieval.

Audley

See Touchet

Bage

B[ENNETT], J.H.E. 'Chester paper manufacturers: Bage family *etc.*', *C.Sf.* 3rd series **49**, 1956. 11. 18-19th c.

Baillier
See Done

Ball
LOWE, A.E.LAWSON. 'Ball of Tussingham and of Boughton', *Reliquary* **11**, 1870-71, 33-4. Includes pedigree, 11-19th c.

Banastre
See Stockport

Banner
See Trafford

Barber
HEYWOOD, PAMELA. 'Serendipity in family history', *F.H.S.C.J.* **19**(4), 1990, 17-24. Barber family; includes pedigree, 18-20th c.

Barlowe
BARLOW, JAMES D. 'Barlows at the Horseshoe Inn, Newbold, Astbury', *F.H.S.C.J.* **22**(4), 1993, 22-3. 19th c.

Barnes
W., H.M. 'Barnes family of Chester', *C.Sf.* 3rd series **28**, 1935, 82-3. 16-17th c.

Barrow
H., T. 'Barrow of Barrow ...', *C.Sf.* 3rd series **3**, 1901, 88-9 & 92-3. 15-16th c.

Baseley
See Duncalf

Basnett
PERCIVAL, S.T.B. 'The Basnetts during the 16th and 17th centuries', *J.C.A.H.S.* **49**, 1962, 27-50. Includes folded pedigrees of Basnett of Dublin and Eyton Uchaf, Denbighshire, 16-18th c., and Basnett of Barnton, Cheshire, 16-19th c.

Bate
'Bate', *Lancashire and Cheshire historian* **1**, 1965, 99, 149-50, 169-70 & 235-6. Extracts from the parish registers of Macclesfield, Over Peover and Mobberley, 19th c., *etc.*

Bateman
HIBBERT, THOMAS DORNING. 'Eight letters relating to Cheshire, of the time of Elizabeth and James I', *H.S.L.C.* **5**, 1853, 118-27. Bateman family letters, 1587-1609.

Bavand
HEWITT, JOHN. 'Bavand family', *C.Sf.* **3**, 1891, 152-3. Medieval-17th c.

Beauchamp
See Mandeville

Beazley
BEAZLEY, F.C. *Pedigree of the family of Beazley.* Mitchell Hughes & Clarke, 1921. Of Alverstoke, Hampshire, Kenley and Wallington, Surrey, and Oxton, Cheshire, 18-20th c.
See also Byseley

Beckett
BECKETT, FRANK D. 'A short history of a Cheshire family', *F.H.S.C.J.* **12**(4), 1983, 11-14. Beckett family, 17-19th c.

Beecroft
See Bostock

Bennett
HANCE, EDWARD M. *Notes on the ancient Cheshire families of Bennett of Saughall Massey, and Bennett of Barnston with their collateral branches.* Liverpool: Thomas Brakell, 1889.
HANCE, E.M. 'Notes on the ancient Cheshire families of Bennett of Saughall Massey, and Bennett of Barnston, with their collateral branches', *H.S.L.C.* **38**; N.S., **2**, 1886, 37-148. See also frontispiece. 14-18th c.
HANCE, EDWARD, W. 'Derivation of the family of Bennett of Barnston', *C.Sf.* 3rd series **11**, 1915, 61-2. 15-17th c.

Bentley
'Bentley: extracts of the name of Bentley from the registers of the parochial chapel of Witton in the County of Chester, from their first commencement in 1561 to 1700', *M.G.H.* N.S., **3**, 1880, 143-4.

Berrington
BENNETT, J.H.E. 'The Berringtons of Cheshire', *J.C.A.H.S.* N.S., **19**, 1912, 125-61. Includes folded pedigree, medieval-17th c.
See also Whittingham

15

Beverley
B[ENNETT], J.H.E. 'Beverley family of Huntington Hall', *C.Sf.* 3rd series **34**, 1941, 99-100. 16-17th c.

Bigland
STALLYBRASS, BILL. *The Biglands of Cheshire.* Yeovil: Linden Hall Publishers, 1988. Includes pedigree, 16-20th c.

Bingley
BELL-JONES, W. 'The Bingleys of Broughton', *C.Sf.* 3rd series **40**, 1948, 85-8, *passim.* Includes extracts from Dodleston register, 16-17th c.
BINGLEY, RANDAL. 'Sir John Bingley and his family', *F.H.S.C.J.* **7**(2), 1978, 7-9. 16-17th c.

Birchenough
BIRCHENOUGH, JOSEPHINE. 'To the manor born', *N.C.F.H.* **19**(1) 1992, 23-5. Birchenough family of Wildboarclough, 17-18th c., includes pedigree.

Birkenhead
GOODACRE. F.B. 'Origin of the Birkenheads of Backford', *C.Sf.* 3rd series **32**, 1938, 33. 15-16th c.

Bisley
See Byseley

Blackburne
R[YLANDS], J.P. 'The Blackburne family of Bridge End, in Latchford, Co. Chester', *C.Sf.* 3rd series **7**, 1910, 27-8, 29-30, 31-2, 35, 38 & 40-41; **8**, 1911, 1. See also 91, & **9**, 1913, 9. 17-18th c., includes parish register extracts, wills, *etc.*

Blinston
COOPER, KATHRYN. 'Some notes on the Blinston family', *Q.J.L.D.* **7**(2), 1984, 6-8. 17-19th c.

Booth
BOOTH, JOHN NICHOLLS. *Booths in history: their roots and lives, encounters and achievements.* Los Alamitos, California: Ridgeway Press, 1982. Of Dunham Massey and the United States; includes pedigree, 13-19th c.

SHERCLIFF, W.H., & SHERCLIFFE, K.N. 'The Booth family of Poynton', *Poynton Local History Society newsletter* **11**, 1985, 2-6. 19-20th c.
SWARBRICK, JOHN. 'Dunham Massey Hall', *L.C.A.S.* **42**, 1925, 53-80. Includes folded pedigree of Booth, 16-19th c.
See also Knottesford

Bordman
RYLANDS, J.PAUL 'The Bordman family, rectors of Grappenhall, Co. Chester', *Lancashire and Cheshire antiquarian notes* **2**, 1886, 58-61. 17-19th c.

Bostock
B[ENNETT], J.H.E. 'The Bostocks of Tattenhall', *C.Sf.* 3rd series **29**, 1935, 32-7, *passim.* 16-17th c., includes wills.
BOSTOCK, ROBERT CHIGNELL. *The family of Bostock of Tarporley, Cheshire.* Ramsgate: S.R.Wilson, 1906. Includes pedigree, 12-19th c.
FRYER, W.V. 'The Bostock family of Cheshire', *C.Sf.* N.S., **1**, 1895, 154-5. See also 188-9 & 191-2.
HIBBERT, LARRY E. 'A general search in Stockport Registration Office nets results', *N.C.F.H.* **15**(2), 1988, 42-4. Bostock and Beecroft families, 19th c.
S[TEWART-]B[ROWN], R. 'Bostock family of Churton and Holt', *C.Sf.* 3rd series **29**, 1935, 27 & 31. 15-17th C.
'Bostock family of Belgrave', *C.Sf.* 3rd series **29**, 1935, 59-60. 16-17th c., includes will of George Bostock, 1610/11.

Bowden
BOWDEN, CHRIS. 'Bowden Index', *Manchester genealogist* **28**(4), 1992, 10-11. Discusses an index to Bowden or Boden references in Derbyshire, Cheshire and Lancashire.

Bozley
B[ENNETT], J.H.E. 'Chester paper manufacturers: Thomas Bozley', *C.Sf.* 3rd series **49**, 1956, 12-13. Includes genealogical notes, 18-19th c.

Bradford
BRADFORD, W.H. 'The Cheshire Bradfords', *C.Sf.* 3rd series **5**, 1904, 101-2 & 107-9. Medieval-20th c. Includes parish register extracts.

Bradshaw

B[ENNETT], J.H.E. 'Alderman Edward Bradshaw of Chester etc.', *C.Sf.* 3rd series **20**, 1924, 79-82. Includes monumental inscriptions and many extracts from the parish registers of St. Peters, Chester, 1633-68.

Brassey

See Radmore

Brentnall

BRENTNALL, J.B. 'Putting leaves on the bare branches of the family tree', *N.C.F.H.* **12**(4), 1985, 107-9. Includes pedigree of Brentnall of Bramshall, 17th c.

Brereton

BROOKE,RICHARD. 'On Handford Old Hall, in Cheshire, formerly the residence of the ancient family of Brereton, with an account of Cheadle church, in that county, and of the monuments of the Breretons in it', *H.S.L.C.* **2**, 1850, 41-54. 16-17th c., includes pedigree of Honford of Handforth, medieval - 17th c.

DWARRIS, SIR FORTUNATUS. *A memoir of the Brereton family, with occassional notices of certain other of the old Cheshire families* J.B. Nicholas and Son, 1848. Includes pedigree, medieval - 19th c.

DWARRIS, FORTUNATUS. 'Observations upon the history of one of the old Cheshire families', *Archaeologia* **33**, 1850, 55-83. Brereton family; medieval.

HEWITT, JOHN. 'The families of Brereton', *C.Sf.* 3rd series **27**, 1934, 12-50, *passim;* **31**, 1937, 61-92, *passim.* 15-18th c.

MOIR, A.L. *The story of Brereton Hall, Cheshire.* 2nd ed. Chester: Phillipson and Golder, 1949. Includes brief descent of the Brereton family, 12-18th c.

MONTAGUE-SMITH, P.W. 'Ancestry of Owen Salusbury Brereton of Shotwick Park', *C.Sf.* 3rd series **45**, 1951, 13. See also 17-18. 17-18th c.

Bridgewater

FALK, BERNARD. *The Bridgewater millions: a candid family history.* Hutchinson & Co., 1942. History of the Dukes of Bridgewater, 17-19th c.

Broadbent

'Broadbent of Acton', *C.Sf.* 3rd series **9**, 1913, 31-2. 16-18th c.

Broadhurst

S., A.G. 'The Broadhurst family and the Bache estates', *C.Sf.* 3rd series **36**, 1948, 54-6, *passim.* 18th c.

'An old Chester lawyer', *C.Sf.* 3rd series **21**, 1926, 89. Broadhurst family, 17th c.

Brock

See Gregg

Brocklehurst

CROZIER, MARY. *An old silk family 1745-1945: the Brocklehursts of Brocklehurst-Whiston Amalgamated Limited.* Aberdeen: Aberdeen University Press, 1947. 18-20th c.

Brooke

HUGHES, T. CANN. 'Brooke of Norton Priory', *Notes and queries* **167**, 1934, 65-66. 17-19th c.

LOCKETT, R.C. 'Richard Brooke Handford vel Handforth and Liverpool, F.S.A., some notes concerning his lineage and connections', *H.S.L.C.* **62**; N.S., **26**, 1910, 175-81. 17-18th c.

W., T.L.O. 'Richard Brook of Handford', *C.Sf.* 3rd series **9**, 1913, 25. Actually gives descent of Brooke of Smallwood.

'Cheshire families: Brooke of Mere', *A.N.Q.* **1**, 1882, 168-9. 16-19th c.

Broughton

'Broughton: entries relating to the family of Broughton copied from the family bible at Doddington', *M.G.H.* N.S., **4**, 1884, 184. 18th c.

Brown

'Captain John Brown', *C.Sf.* 3rd series **15**, 1920. 57. See also **16**, 1921, 1-2. Extracts from family prayer book and bible, 18th c., of Chester.

Browne

WILLIAMS, CHARLES. 'The pedigree of Sir Thomas Browne', *Norfolk archaeology* **15**, 1904, 109-13. 16-19th c., of Cheshire and Norfolk.

Brownell
STAVERT, W.S. 'The Brownells of Gawsworth',
C.Sf. 3rd series **2**, 1898, 92-3, 97-8 & 101-3.
16-18th c., includes parish register abstracts
and monumental inscriptions.

Bruce
See Duncalf

Bruen
P., W.T. 'The Bruen family of Cheshire', *C.Sf.*
N.S., **1**, 1895, 115-6. See also 86 & 90. Bruen
and Longford families, 17th c.
'Bruen and Longford families', *C.Sf.* 3rd series
48, 1956, 48-9 & 50. 18th c.

Brus
See Chester, Earls of

Bulkeley
GENEALOGIST. 'How to write the history of a
family', *C.N.Q.* **8**, 1888, 226-9. Includes
pedigree of Bulkeley of Cheadle and
Beaumaris, Anglesea, 17-18th c.
'Pedigree of Bulkeley of Cheshire and Ireland,
Wales, Salop and Bedford', *New England
historical and genealogical register* **23**, 1869,
300-304. Medieval.

Bullock
BULLOCK, MICHAEL. 'Migration in nineteenth
century Cheshire', *F.H.S.C.J.* **21**(4), 1992,
11-14. Bullock family, 19th c.

Bunbury
S[TEWART]-B[ROWN] R. 'The Bunbury family of
Bunbury and Stanney at Wrexham', *C.Sf.* 3rd
series **24**, 1929. 17th c.

Bushell
WHITEBROOK, J.C. 'Bushell of Frodsham',
Congregational History Society transactions
6, 1913-15, 379-88. Includes folded pedigree,
17th c.

Byseley
BEAZLEY, F.C. *Pedigree of Byseley, Bisley or
Beazley, of Newington and Warborough, Co.
Oxon., Ryde and Alverstoke, Co.
Southampton, and Oxton, Co. Chester.*
Mitchell Hughes and Clarke, 1928. Reprinted
from *M.G.H.*, 5th series **6**, 1926-8, 390-408.
16-20th c.

Caldwell
See Minshull

Callcott
HUGHES, RICHARD. 'Two centuries of Callcotts',
Malpas history **7**, 1986, 8-11. Includes
pedigree, 18-19th c.

Calveley
'Calveley and Davenport families', *C.Sf.* 3rd
series **15**, 1920, 15-16. Extracts from Bunbury
parish register, 16-18th c.

Chadwick
LANE, D. 'A Chadwick family of Stockport and
Warwick', *Manchester genealogist* **30**(2), 1994,
30-34. 19th c.

Chester, Earls of
MORTIMER, W.WILLIAMS. 'Memoir of the Earls
of Chester, part II: the Norman earls',
H.S.L.C. **4**, 1952, 85-97.
PLANCHE, J.R. 'On the seals of the Earls of
Chester', *Journal of the British
Archaeological Assocation* **5**, 1850, 235-52.
Includes genealogical notes.
STEWART-BROWN, R. 'Abeyance of title as
illustrated by the Earldom of Chester case',
Genealogist N.S., **36**, 1920, 169-73. Medieval.
SLEIGH, JOHN. 'Norman Earls Palatine of
Cheshire', *Reliquary* **9**, 1868-9, 79-80. Includes
pedigree of Meschines, Brus, *etc.*, medieval.

Chetwood
TUCKER, STEPHEN *Pedigree of the family
Chetwode of Chetwode, Co. Bucks, of Oakley,
Co. Stafford, Worleston, Co.Chester, and of
Warkworth, Co. Northampton, with their
charters and other evidences, to which is
added report and papers connected with their
claim to the Barony of De Wahull, and an
account of the Chetwode Rhyne.* Mitchell &
Hughes, 1884. Includes pedigrees, medieval-
18th c., wills, deed, monumental inscriptions,
parish register extracts, *etc.*
'The true pedegree & descent of ye auntient &
right worshipful familie of Chetwood of
Chetwood, & Warleston, Hoclyue,
Warkeworth, as they are descended from the
most anrcient barons of Wahull alias
Woodhull in the County of Bedford, & Leon
in the countie of Northampton ...', *M.G.H.* 2nd
series **1**, 1886, 69-88. 11-18th c.

18

Cholmondley

'Christening the Cholmondley children', *Journal of the Knutsford Historical and Archaeological Association* 1(6), 1980, 8-10. 18-19th c.

Church

BULLOCK, CONSTANCE. 'The family of Church of Nantwich', *F.H.S.C.J.* 10(2), 1980, 15-16; 10(3), 1981, 6. 16-17th c.

Churche's Mansion, Nantwich, Cheshire: the historic Tudor home of the Churche family: a merchant's house restored and rehabilitated. Derby: English Life publication 1957. Includes brief pedigree of Churche, 16-20th c.

Clayton

PRIDDLE, PAT. 'Unravelling those Claytons', *N.C.F.H.* 18(4), 1991, 100-103. Includes pedigree, 18-19th c. of Cheshire and Derbyshire.

RYLANDS, J.PAUL. 'The Claytons, of Thelwall and Sheepcroft, Co. Chester; of St. Dominick's Abbey and Doneraile, Co Cork', *H.S.L.C.* 32, 1880, 35-52. See also iii. 13-18th c.

RYLANDS, JOHN PAUL. *Some account of the Clayton family of Thelwell, Co. Chester, afterwards of St. Dominick's Abbey, Doneraile, and Mallow, Co. Cork.* Liverpool: T.Brakell, 1880 14-17th c.

R[YLANDS], J.P. 'The Clayton family of Thelwall', *C.Sf.* 3rd series 14, 1919, 43-4. Includes extracts from Grappenhall parish register, 16-17th c.

RYLEY, PAUL. 'Migration and occupation: Clayton of Poynton', *N.C.F.H.* 15(1), 1988, 4-7. 18-19th c., includes pedigree.

Cobbe

ANGEL, CERI. 'The Cobbes of Wybunbury', *F.H.S.C.J.* 18(2), 1988, 16-18. Includes pedigree, 17-20th c.

Coffin

See Rowe

Colley

DAVIES-COLLEY, T.H. *The family of Colley of Churton Heath in the County of Chester, with some pedigrees of related families,* ed. W.F. Irvine. Ballantyne Press, 1931. Medieval-

19th c., includes pedigrees of Davies, Denton, Dutton, Harrison and Jackson. (some folded)

Cornwall-Legh

LORD, EVELYN. 'The Cornwall-Leghs of High Legh: approaches to the inheritance patterns of North-West England', *Bulletin of the John Rylands University Library of Manchester* 73(2), 1991, 21-36. Includes pedigree, 13-20th c.

RICHARDS, RAYMOND. 'The chapels of the Blessed Virgin Mary and St. John at High Legh, Cheshire, with some account of the Cornwall-Legh and Egerton-Legh families', *H.S.L.C.* 101, 1949, 97-136. Includes folded pedigree of Legh of High Legh, medieval - 19th c.

Cotgrave

'The Cotgrave family', *C.Sf.* 3rd series 4, 1903, 39-41, 47-9, 65-6, 88-9, 117-88 & 122-3. Medieval-18th c.

'The Cotgrave family', *C.Sf.* 3rd series 5, 1904, 94-5. Medieval.

Cotgreave

STEWART-BROWN, R. 'The Cotgreave pedigree forgeries', *Genealogists' magazine* 6, 1932-4, 288-93. See also 370. 18-19th c.

Cottingham

COTTINGHAM, E.R. 'Notes on the Cottinghams of Chester', *C.Sf.* 3rd series 14, 1919, 61-2. See also 63-4, & 20, 1924, 56. 15-17th c.

C[OTTINGHAM], E.R. 'Pedigree of the family of Cottingham of Chester and Ledsham', *C.Sf.* 3rd series 20, 1924, 98-9. 15-17th c.

COTTINGHAM, E.R. 'Pedigree of the family of Cottingham of Chester and Ledsham', *C.Sf.* 3rd series 22, 1926, 10-11. 17th c.

Crewe

CARTER,WILLIAM F. 'The early Crewe pedigree', *Genealogist* N.S., 37, 1921, 113-27 & 174-83. Medieval.

L., V. 'The family of Crewe of Crewe', *C.Sf.* 3rd series 30, 1935, 23.

R[YLANDS], J.P. 'The family of Crewe of Crewe', *C.S.F.* 3rd series 12, 1917, 67-8, 69-70 & 71-2. 16-17th c.

'Crewe family of Bolesworth', *C.Sf.* 3rd series 16, 1921, 534. 18th c.

See also Done

Cromwell

CROMWELL, L. 'Cromwell', *Lancashire and Cheshire historian* **1**, 1966, 269-70. 19th c.

Crowther

'The late Rev. J.H.L. Crowther', *C.N.Q.* N.S., **2**, 1897, 195-6. Includes Crowther/Crowder extracts from Stockport parish register, 17-19th c.

Cyveliock

See Audley

Danyers

RYLANDS, J.PAUL. 'A vellum pedigree-roll of the family of Danyers *alias* Danyell, of the County of Chester', *Genealogist* N.S., **32**, 1916, 7-19. 13-17th c.

Davenport

DAVENPORT, AMZI BENEDICT. *A history and genealogy of the Davenport family in England and America from AD 1086 to 1850 . . .* New York: S.W. Benedict, 1851. Supplement, 1876. Medieval-19th c., primarily concerned with the American branch of the family from the 16th c. Supplement includes extensive pedigree, 12-19th c.

HIGHET, T.P., ed. *The early history of the Davenports of Davenport.* Cm.S., 3rd series **9**. 1960. Medieval; includes deeds.

'Pedigree of Davenport', *New England historical & genealogical register* **9**, 1855, 146-8. Medieval-19th c., of Davenport, Cheshire, Coventry, Warwickshire, and the United States.

SILKE, MARGARET. 'The Tudor Davenports of Bramal', *North West Catholic history* **1972-3**, 52-95.

See also Calveley

Davies

See Colley

Day

GENEALOGIST. 'Day family of Frankby and Newton *cum* Larton', *C.Sf.* 3rd series **29**, 1935, 6-7. See also 13-14. 16-18th c.

Dedwood

B[ENNETT], J.H.E. 'The Dedwoods of Chester and their mansion', *C.Sf.* 3rd series **22**, 1927, 65-77, *passim.* Medieval.

Delamere

DELAMERE, B., & LANGLEY, C.E. 'Forbears and descendants of Daniel Delamere, yeoman, 1712-97', *F.H.S.C.J.* **8**(3), 1979, 11-12; **8**(4), 1979, 9-11.

Delves

BROUGHTON, SIR DELVES L. *Records of an old Cheshire family: a history of the lords of the manors of Delves, near Uttoxeter in the County of Stafford, & Doddington in the County of Chester.* A. Fairbairns & Co., 1908. Delves and Broughton families, 13-19th c., includes pedigrees.

Denton

See Colley

Dod

DOD, O.C.WOOLLEY. 'The family of Dod of Edge in the County of Chester', *C.Sf.* 3rd series **32**, 1938, 98-9, 100-110, *passim;* **33**, 1939, 3-55, *passim.* Medieval-19th c.

JONES, R. WILBRAHAM. 'Dod family of Shocklach: testamur of descent', *C.Sf.* **1**, 1878, 55. 17th c.

Doe

'The Doe family of Little Saughall', *C.Sf.* 3rd series **50**, 1958, 39. 17-18th c.

Dodge

W[ILD], W.I. 'An old Stockport family, some interesting notes', *C.N.Q.* N.S., **2**, 1897, 17-19. Dodge family; includes extracts from parish registers, 16-17th c.

Done

CASH, SARAH. 'The Dones of Utkinton', *C.N.Q.* N.S., **2**, 1897, 163-6 & 256-65; **3**, 1898, 83-7, 121-3 & 172-5; **4**, 1899, 18-21.

FERGUSSON, R.S. 'Roll of the hereditary chief foresters, master foresters, masters of the game and bowbearers-in-chief of the forests of Mara and Modrem [Delamere Forest]', *C.Sf.* 4th series **3**, 1968, 21-2. Descent through Done, Crewe, Arderne, BaillieHamilton, and O'Brien, medieval-20th c.

Drinkwater

DRINKWATER, C.H., & FLETCHER, W.G.D. *The family of Drinkwater, of Cheshire,*

Lancashire, the Isle of Man, etc. Fleet:
E.Dwelly, 1920. Includes pedigrees,
17-19th c.

Dukinfield
RYLANDS, J. PAUL. 'A vellum pedigree of the
families of Dukinfield, Co. Chester, and
Holland of Denton, Co. Lancaster, drawn in
the year 1622', *Genealogist* N.S., **32**, 1916, 85-
90. 13-17th c.

Duncalf
COLE, ANNE 'The Duncalf-Baseley connection',
F.H.S.C.J. **20**(2), 1990, 12-16. 19th c.
COLE, ANNE. 'The Duncalf-Bruce connection: a
one name study problem', *F.H.S.C.J.* **17**(3),
1988, 15-17. 18-19th c.

Dunstan
COOK, N.P. 'John Dunstan and his family (1798-
1874)', *Cheshire history* **21**, 1988, 34-6.

Dutton
*Memorials of the Duttons of Dutton in
Cheshire, with notes respecting the
Sherborne branch of the family.* London:
Henry Sotheran & Co., Chester: Minshull &
Meeson, 1901. Medieval-19th c., includes
pedigrees (some folded) with many extracts
from original sources.
See also Colley

Eachus
EACHUS, FRED. W. 'A branch of the Eachus
family, Church Minshall', *N.C.F.H.* **4**(3),
1977, 72-5. 18-20th c.

Earle
EARLE, T. ALGERNON. 'Earle of Allerton Tower',
H.S.L.C. **42**, N.S., **6**, 1892, 15-76. Includes
pedigrees, 16-19th c., extracts from parish
registers, *etc.* Also of Frodsham, Cheshire.

Edgcombe
'Edward [Edgcombe] of Tewkesbury and
Ellesmere', *Edgcombe family genealogy and
history* **8**, 1990, 183-7. 18-20th c. descent.

Edwards
STEWART-BROWN, R. 'Edwards of Chirk, Co.
Denbigh, and of Cheveley, Co. Chester', *C.Sf.*
3rd series **17**, 1922, 15-25, *passim.* 16-17th c.

Egerton
BEAMONT, WILLIAM. 'On marriage contracts,
with remarks on an Egerton marriage
settlement, dated 10 Henry VI', *Journal of
the Architectural, Archaeological and
Historic Society for ... Chester* **1**(6), 1861,
183-202. Includes medieval Egerton
pedigree.
CHORLTON, R.G. 'The Egertons of Tatton Park,
Knutsford', *Lancashire and Cheshire
historian* **2**, 1966, 458. 18th c.,
'Cheshire families: Egerton of Tatton', *A.N.Q.*
1, 1882, 149-51. 16-19th c.
'The Egerton family', *A.N.Q.* **3**, 1883,
supplement, iii-xii. 13-17th c.

Egerton-Leigh
See Cornwall-Legh

Ellame
'Ellames family', *C.Sf.* 3rd series **55**, 1960, 2.
See also 26, 34-5 & 66-7. 19th c.

Etchells
CRUICKSHANK, DURWARD. 'One path through
sources', *N.C.F.H.* **15**(2), 1988, 35-8. Etchells
family, 16-18th c.

Fawsitt
See Hartley

Finney
FINNEY, SAMUEL. 'Memoirs of the family of
Finney of Finney, of Fulshaw (near
Wilmslow) Cheshire', *Cheshire & Lancashire
historical collector* **1**, 1853, 49-53, 61-66, 75-7,
85-8, 97-103 & 109-11. 16-18th c.
'Pedigree of the family of Finney, of Fulshaw,
Cheshire', *Cheshire and Lancashire
historical collector* **2**, 1855, 107-9. Medieval-
18th c.

Fitton
E., H.G. 'The Fitton of Gawsworth', *C.N.Q.* N.S.,
1, 1896, 81-2. 17th c.

Fitz Geoffrey
See Mandeville

Fitz-Roger
See Stokeport

21

Fletcher
See Pickering

Foden
See Hurdsfield

Foliott
BEWLEY, EDMUND T. 'The Foliotts of Londonderry and Chester', *Genealogist* N.S., **20**, 1904, 108-13. 17-19th c.
'The Folliott family', *C.Sf.* 3rd series **29**, 1935, 3-4. Of Chester; early 19th c.

Francis
L., P.H. 'Francis family of Childer Thornton', *C.Sf.* 3rd series **32**, 1938, 42-3 & 45. 16-17th c.

Gandy
R., G.G. 'Gandy family of Higher Lymm Booths', *C.Sf.* 3rd series **18**, 1923, 9-10. 17-18th c.

Garratt
See Heath

Gatliff
R[YLANDS], J.P. 'Gatliff family of Walton, Co. Chester', *C.Sf.* 3rd series **18**, 1923, 27. 18th c.

Gerard
RYLANDS, J. PAUL. 'A pedigree of the family of Gerard of Crewood, Frodsham, &c., in the County of Chester, drawn by Randle Holme of Chester in 1691, and descent continued in the family of Perryn of Trafford Hall in the same county, about 1840', *Genealogist* N.S., **30**, 1914, 205-7. Medieval-19th c.

Gernet
See Stokeport

Gibbons
GIBBON, EDWARD. *Some Cheshire Gibbons: a family history.* Church Stretton: the author, 1972. Includes folded pedigree, 18-20th c.

Gilbert
'Gilbert family of Woodbank and Chester', *C.Sf.* 3rd series **36**, 1948. 63-4 & 68. 16-18th c.

Gleave
GLEAVE, SYDNEY. 'My genealogical struggle', *N.C.F.H.* **11**(3), 1984, 69-71. Gleave family, 19th c.

Glegg
HISTORICUS. 'The origin of the family of Glegg of Gayton', *C.Sf.* 3rd series **39**, 1948, 58-9. Medieval.
'The Gleggs of Gayton in Wirral', *C.Sf.* 3rd series **53**, 1938, 28-34, *passim.* Includes will of John Glegg, 1619/20.

Greene
See Lancelyn

Greenwell
SHERCLIFF, W.H. 'The Greenwells and Poynton', *Poynton Local History Society newsletter* **10**, 1985, 7-16. 19-20th.

Greg
ROSE, MARY B. *The Gregs of Quarry Bank Mill: the rise and decline of a family firm.* Cambridge University Press, 1986. Includes pedigrees 18-20th c.
ROSE, MARY B. *The Gregs of Styal.* [Styal]: Quarry Bank Mill Development Trust, 1978. Includes pedigree, 18-20th c.
'The Gregs of Styal', *C.N.Q.* N.S., **8**, 1908-11, 66-72. 18-19th c.

Gregg
TWEMLOW, FRAS.R. 'Gregg of Bradley in Appleton, and Brock of Upton. *C.Sf.* 3rd series **11**, 1915, 8, 10-11 & 12. See also 17. Includes pedigree. 17-18th c.

Gregge
'Gregge and Holt families of Cheshire and Lancashire', *P.N.* **4**, 1884, 237-8. Includes brief pedigree, 17-18th c.

Grosvenour
'The Grosvenours of Hulme', *C.Sf.* 3rd series **3**, 1901, 140-43. Medieval.

Haddock
McKENNA, DON. 'Haddock of Halton', *F.H.S.C.J.* **23**(2), 1993, 12-15; **23**(3), 1994, 17-21. 19-20th c.

22

Hague

CARR, PHILIP,H. 'The Hagues of Dukinfield and Ashton', *N.C.F.H.* 9(2), 38-40. 18th c.

GOLDIE, E. 'The search for my ancestors: the Hagues of Mellor', *N.C.F.H.* 8(4), 1981, 98-103.

Hamilton

See Done

Hampson

HULLAND, JESSIE HAMPSON. 'The Hampsons of Lostock Hall Farm', *Poynton Local History Society newsletter* 9, 1984, 15-16. 18-19th c.

Hanford

See Brereton

Hankey

JONES, MERRILL. 'Offered, one family Bible', *F.H.S.C.J.* 12(2), 1982, 9. Lists entries in the Hankey family's bible, 19th c.

Hardware

GLASGOW, ROBERTA. *The Hardwares of Cheshire, an 18th century letter edited and explained.* Liverpool: T. Brokell, 1948. 16-18th c., includes brief pedigrees.

Harper

B[ENNETT], J.H.E. 'The Harpers of Stockport', *C.Sf.* 3rd series 7, 1910, 81-2. 17th c.

Harpur

X. 'Harpur family of Chester', *C.Sf.* 3rd series 35, 1948, 16-30, *passim.*

Harrison

B[ENNETT], F.C. 'Richard Harrison of West Kirby and afterwards of New England', *C.Sf.* 3rd series 25, 1931, 46-51, *passim.* Includes genealogical notes.
See also Colley

Hartley

TURNER, M. 'Treasure from a market stall', *F.H.S.C.J.* 12(2), 1982, 4-6. Lists photographs from a family album, mainly relating to the Hartley and Fawsitt families. Many names.

Hatton

HELSBY, T. 'Baptisms, marriages and burials of the Hattons of Hatton, *juxta* Daresbury in Cheshire', *Reliquary* 15, 1874-5, 221-4.

Hazlehurst

BUCKLER, J.F. 'The name Hazlehurst', *Wirral notes and queries* 1, 1892, 19-20. Includes extracts from Birkenhead parish register, 18-19th c.

Heap

TOMPKINS, MURIEL HEAP. 'Heaps and heaps of Heaps', *F.H.S.C.J.* 13(1), 3-6. 18-19th c.

HEAPE, CHARLES, HEAPE, RICHARD. *Records of the family of Heape of Heape, Staley, Saddleworth and Rochdale, from circa 1170 to 1905.* Rochdale: Aldine Press, 1905. Includes pedigrees (some folded) and many extracts from original sources.

Heath

LIVESEY, J. 'Heath family of Baddington, in the parish of Acton', *C.Sf.* 3rd series 22, 1927, 40-41. Includes will of Joseph Garratt of Bramhall, 1812 (proved 1814).

L[IVESEY] J. 'Heath family of Cheshire', *C.Sf.* 3rd series 12-15, 1917-20, *passim.* 17-18th c., includes wills.

READE, ALLEN LYELL. 'The origin of the Heath family of Titherington', *C.Sf.* 3rd series 17, 1922, 11-12. See also 20, 1924, 41. 17-18th c., originally of Leek, Staffordshire. Includes wills.

Helsby

HOWARD, J. JACKSON, ed. *The pedigree, descent or genealogy of the ancient and worshipful house of Helsby, lords of Helsby, Chorlton, and Acton, in the county palatine of Chester* . . . Taylor & Co., 1868. Medieval-18th c., includes extracts from Frodsham parish register.

'Extracts from the registers of the parish church of Frodsham relating to the family of Helsby of Helsby and Kingsley, Co. Chester', *M.G.H.* 1, 1874, 91-4. 16-18th c.

Henry

CRAWFORD, PATRICIA. 'Katherine and Philip Henry and their children: a case study in family ideology', *H.S.L.C.* 134, 1985, 39-73. 17th c., includes pedigree.

Henry *continued*
V., B.L.L. 'The Henrys', *C.Sf.* 2, 1883, 22-3.
17th c.

Higginbottom
The Higginbottom family bulletin. Canterbury:
Frank Higginbottom, 1970-81. Includes many
articles of Lancashire and Cheshire interest
not otherwise listed here.

Hockenhull
'The Hockenhulls of Hockenhull and Shotwick',
C.Sf. 3rd series 19, 1924, 85.
See also Ravenshaw

Holcroft
B., J. 'Holcroft of Vale Royal', *C.Sf.* 3rd series
12, 1917, 7-15, *passim.* 16-17th c., includes
wills.
RYLANDS, JOHN PAUL. *Notes on the families of
Holcroft, of Holcroft, Co. Lancaster;
Holcroft of Vale Royal, Co. Chester.,
Holcroft of Hurst, Co. Lancaster, Holcroft of
East Ham, Co. Essex, Holcroft of Bolderton,
Co. Notts., Holcroft of Basingstoke, Co.
Hants., etc., with an account of their arms.*
Leigh: Josiah Rose, 1877. Medieval-
18th c.

Holes
'An ancient Cheshire family', *C.Sf.* 3rd series
5, 1904, 77-80. Holes or Hollis family,
14-17th c.

Holland
IRVINE, WM. FERGUSSON, ed. *A history of the
family of Holland of Mobberley and
Knutsford in the County of Chester, with
some account of the family of Holland of
Upholland and Denton in the County of
Lancaster, from materials collected by the
late Edgar Swinton Holland.* Edinburgh:
Ballantyne Press, 1902. Includes deed
abstracts, extracts from parish registers,
folded pedigrees, 13-19th c., *etc.*
RYLANDS, J.PAUL. 'A pedigree of the family of
Holland of Mobberley in the County of
Chester, drawn about the year 1650',
Genealogist N.S., 31, 1915, 93-5. 15-17th c.

Hollis
See Holes

Holmes
EARWAKER, J.P. 'The four Randle Holmes, of
Chester, antiquaries, heralds and genealogists,
c.1571 to 1707', *J.C.A.H.S.* N.S., 4, 1892, 113-70.
Includes folded pedigree, 17-18th c., also
notes on their antiquarian manuscripts.
MORTIMER, I. WILLIAMS. 'Memoir of the family
of Holme, especially of the various Randle
Holmes, the Cheshire antiquaries of the
seventeenth century', *H.S.L.C.* 1, 1849, 86-94.
TAYLOR, HENRY. 'On the discovery of three
documents furnishing additional evidence
relating to the family of the Randle Holmes,
of Chester', *J.C.A.H.S.* N.S., 16(2), 1909, 26-35.
17-18th c.

Holt
HOLT, BARBARA. 'The house of Holt in
Bramhall', *N.C.F.H.* 21(3), 1994, 75-82.
17-19th c.
See also Gregge

Hulley
HULLEY, RAY. 'The history and families of the
One House, Rainow, *N.C.F.H.* 18(2), 1991, 35-
40; 18(3), 1991, 86-9. Hulley family. Medieval-
20th c.

Hulme
OWEN, J. 'Hulme and Strettle families', *A.N.Q.*
3, 1883, 146-7. Of Manchester and Mobberley,
includes parish register extracts, 16-18th c.

Hurdsfield
HALL, J.R. 'The Hurdsfield-Foden legend',
N.C.F.H. 15(3), 1988, 72-5. 17-19th c.

Ithell
B[ENNETT], J.H.E. 'Ithell family of Upton by
Chester', *C.Sf.* 3rd series 38, 1948, 52-3.
16-18th c.

Jackson
MASTERS, R.S. 'My family and the Primitive
Methodist connection', *F.H.S.C.J.* 8(1), 1978,
11-12. Jackson family, 19th c.
See also Colley

Janney
WHITE, MILES. 'The Quaker Janneys of Cheshire
and their progenitors', *Publications of the
Southern History Association* 8, 1904, 119-28,

196-211 & 275-86. 16-18th c., includes tables of births, marriages and deaths, with folded pedigree.

Jones
See Maddock

Keen
See Pickering

Kelly
LAND, MARY. 'Family history: beginners luck', *J.L.D.L.H.S.* 1(2), 1985, 16-17. Kelly family, 18-19th c.

Kenna
B[ENNETT], J.H.E. 'The Kennas: an innkeeper family of Chester', *C.Sf.* 3rd series **37**, 1948, 35-7. 17-18th c.

Kennerley
'The Cheshire family of Kennerley or Kenworthy', *C.Sf.* 3rd series **52**, 1957, 13-14. 16-17th c.

Kenworthy
See Kennerley

Knottesford
'Knottesford and Booth of Twemlowe', *F.H.S.C.J.* 6(3) 1977. Pedigree facsimile inside cover, medieval-19th c.

Lancelyn
GREEN, ROGER LANCELYN. *Poulton-Lancelyn: the story of an ancestral home.* Oxford: Oxonian Press, 1948. Includes pedigrees of Lancelyn, Greene, and Parnell, medieval-18th c.
OLIVER, V.L. 'Langford family of Tranmere', *C.Sf.* 3rd series **10**, 1914, 13-14. 17th c.
See also Bruen

Larden
B[ENNETT], J.H.E. 'Frog Hall, Tattenhall', *C.Sf.* 3rd series **17**, 1927, 76-7. See also 82. Larden family, 17-19th c.

Latham
ROBINSON, GILLIAN. 'My Latham and Molyneaux ancestors', *F.H.S.C.J.* **20**(1), 1990, 27-9. 19th c.

'Cheshire families: Latham of Bradwall', *A.N.Q.* **1**, 1882, 145. 16-18th c.

Lawrence
'The Lawrence family of Wem and Nantwich', *P.N.* **2**, 1882, 96-100. Includes pedigree, 18th c,

Lea
See Lee

Leadbetter
LEADBEATER, GEOFFREY W. 'The Leadbetters of Sandbach', *F.H.S.C.J.* **18**(3), 1989, 18-23. 19th c.

Lee
LEE, RUPERT HENRY MELVILLE. *Related to Lee.* 3 pts. Oxford: the author, 1963-4. Of Buckinghamshire, Oxfordshire, and Cheshire, *etc.,* medieval-20th c.
'Lee or Lea, of Lee in Wybunbury parish', *C.Sf.* 3rd series **12**, 1917, 25-6. 16th c.

Legh
BEAMONT, W. *A history of the house of Lyme (in Cheshire) compiled from documents of the Legh family of that house, and from other sources.* Warrington: P. Pearse, 1876. Medieval-20th c. Includes folded pedigrees of various related families.
L., F.DE. 'Legh of Lyme', *C.Sf.* 3rd series **14**, 1919, 29. 15-17th c.
NEWTON, LADY E. *The house of Lyme, from its foundation to the end of the eighteenth century.* William Heinemann, 1917. Leigh family, medieval - 18th c.
NEWTON, LADY. *Lyme letters, 1660-1760.* William Heinemann, 1825. Legh family.
L., P.H. 'Rev. Peter Leigh, rector of Aldford, 1677-1727', *C.Sf.* 3rd series **12**, 1917, 49-61, *passim.* Includes wills of Edward Leigh, 1660 and Peter Leigh, 1727, also notes on Minshull, 18th c.
RENAUD, FRANK 'A narrative covering two castellated manor houses formerly existing in Macclesfield with a corresponding chapter of Cheshire history', *L.C.A.S.* **20**, 1902, 119-28. Legh and Macclesfield families, medieval; includes pedigree of Macclesfield to 17th c.

Legh *continued*

RYLANDS, J. PAUL. 'Legh of Norbury Booths Hall, Cheshire', *M.G.H.* 4th series 1, 1906, 135-6. Family notes from a devotional book, 18-19th c.

'Cheshire families: Legh of Addington', *A.N.Q.* 1, 1882, 186-9. Medieval-19th c.

'Legh of Lyme', *C.N.Q.* N.S., 3, 1898, 163-72. 14-19th c.

See also Cornwall-Legh

Leicester

S[TEWART]-B[ROWN], R. 'Leicester family of Hale Lowe and Pickmere', *C.Sf.* 3rd series 17, 1922, 17-18. 16-20th c.

COTTON, B.D., & BORAM, J.M. 'The Leicesters of Macclesfield: a 19th century dynasty of vernacular chair makers', *Cheshire history* 13, 1984, 7-12. Includes pedigree.

Leigh

LEA, G. 'Leigh family of Bickerton', *C.Sf.* 3rd series 32, 1938, 36. See also 38. 16-17th c.

Levesley

'Levesley family of Chester', *C.Sf.* 3rd series 8, 1911, 27, 29, 31, 33, & 35. 16-17th c., includes will of Robert Levesley, 1637.

Lewis

'Lewis family of Chester', *C.Sf.* 3rd series 12, 1917, 81, 834 & 85-6. See also 14, 1919, 80. 16-18th c., includes wills.

Leycester

M., T.J. 'The Leycesters of Worleston, Pool and Chester', *N.C.F.H.* 2, 1883, 85-6 & 89-90. 17-18th c.

'Cheshire families: Leycester of Toft', *A.N.Q.* 1 1882, 126-8. Medieval-19th c.

See also Mainwaring

Lilley

'Lilley family of Chester', *C.Sf.* 3rd series 27, 1934, 5-6. See also 10-11. 15th c.

Lingard

'Whose family', *N.C.F.H.* 4(4) 1977, 116. Extracts from the bible of the Lingard family of Stockport and Manchester, early 19th c.

Lomas

COOK, E.M., *et al.* 'Lomas family genealogies', *Lancashire and Cheshire historian* 1, 1965, 11-14, 29-30, 57-8, 77-8 & 105-6. See also 2, 1966, 285. Of Gawsworth, 18-19th c.

Longford

See Bruen

Lowe

LOWE, ALFRED EDWARD LAWSON. *Some account of the family of Lowe, formerly of Hartford and elsewhere in the County of Chester, subsequently of Highfield in the County of Nottingham, and now of Shirenewton Hall in the County of Monmouth,* ed. Otto William Braunsdorff. Dresden: [ ], 1896. Includes pedigrees (some folded), 15-19th c.

'Pedigree of the family of Lowe, or La Lowe, in the County of Chester, and of Alderwasley, Owlgrave, Hazlewood, Denby, Park Hall, and Locks Park, in the County of Derby and elsewhere', *Reliquary* 11, 1870-71, 254. 15-19th c.

Lowndes

LOWNDES, WILLIAM. *A Cheshire family: Lowndes of Overton, the story of a search.* Bures, Suffolk: William Lowndes, 1972. Includes pedigrees, 11-20th c.

Lymme

See Statham

Macclesfield

MAXFIELD, DAVID K. 'How the Macclesfields left Cheshire in the reign of Henry VI', *Cheshire history* 27, 1991, 10-14.

See also Legh

Macklin

B[ENNETT], J.H.E. 'The Macklins of Storeton, etc., *C.Sf.* 3rd series 34, 1941, 79-80. 18th c.

Maddock

L., P.H. 'Maddock of Chester, and Jones, *C.Sf.* 3rd series 9, 1913, 58-9. 18th c.

Mainwaring

DRIVER, J.T. 'The Mainwarings of Over Peover, a Cheshire family in the fifteenth and early sixteenth centuries', *J.C.A.H.S.* 57, 1974, 27-40. Includes pedigree.

FINLEY, R. MAINWARING. *A short history of the Mainwaring family.* Griffith, Farran, Okeden & Welsh, 1890. Reprinted Research Publishing, 1976. Medieval-19th c., of Over Peover, Cheshire, Whitmore, Staffordshire, Oteley Park, Shropshire, *etc.*

KANDEL, EDWARD M. 'A Cheshire feud', *Coat of arms* N.S., **37**(109), 1979, 129-33. Mainwaring and Leycester families, includes pedigree of Leycester, 13-17th c..

MONTAGUE-SMITH, PATRICK W. KANDEL, EDWARD M. 'A Cheshire feud', *South Cheshire Family History Society quarterly journal* **9**, 1992, 10-13. Mainwaring and Leycester families; includes pedigree, 13-17th c.

'Mainwaring of Kermincham', *C.Sf.* 3rd series **12**, 1917, 79. Pedigree, 17th c.

'Mainwaring of Nantwich', *C.Sf.* 3rd series **12**, 1917, 27-8. 17th c.

'Mainwaring of Newton', *C.Sf.* 3rd series **12**, 1917, 87. 17th c.

'Mainwaring of Peover', *C.Sf.* 3rd series **12**, 1917, 44. Pedigree, 17th c.

Mallory

'The Mallory family of Mobberley', *C.N.Q.* N.S., **8**, 1908-11, 129-39. 16-17th c.

Malpas

SWETTENHAM, SIR ALEXANDER. 'The Barony of Malpas', *Genealogist* N.S., **32**, 1916, 83-4. 11-12th c.

Mandeville

FOWLER, G. HERBERT. 'Mandeville, Fitz Geoffrey, and Beauchamp of Eaton', *Genealogist* N.S., **29**, 1913, 78-85. Includes pedigree, 12-13th c.

Manley

B[ENNETT], J.H.E. 'The Manleys of Lache Hall', *C.Sf.* 3rd series **49**, 1956, 23-34, *passim.* 16-18th c.

Marshall

IREDALE, D.A. 'The rise and fall of the Marshalls of Northwich, salt proprietors: a saga of the industrial era in Cheshire, 1720-1917', *H.S.L.C.* **117**, 1965, 59-82.

Massey

B[EAZLEY], F.C. 'Massey family of Audlem and Denfield', *C.Sf.* 3rd series **8**, 1911, 52-3 & 55. 16-18th c.

B[EAZLEY]. F.C. 'Notes on the pedigree of Massey of Sale', *C.Sf.* 3rd series **10**, 1914, 110. 17th c.

H., J. 'The Mascys of Tatton', *C.Sf.* **2**, 1883, 42-3. 15th c.

MASSEY, FRANK A. *My Massey family in England.* Fort Worth: the author, 1974. See also his *Massey genealogy addendum,* 1979. Medieval-17th c., includes pedigrees.

See also Tillesley

Mere

See Neuton

Meschines

See Chester, Earls of

Middleton

B[ENNETT], J.H.E. 'Middleton and Norris families', *C.Sf.* 3rd series **13**, 1918, 8. 15-16th c.

Minshull

LEGA-WEEKES, ETHEL. 'The families of Minshull of Penketh and Torbock, and Caldwell of Sutton', *C.Sf.* 3rd series **3**, 1901, 97. See also 119-21 & 130. 17-18th c.

L., P.H. 'Richard Mynshull of Chester', *C.Sf.* 3rd series **12**, 1917, 21. See also 70 & 72. 17-18th c.

L., P.H. 'The visitation of Cheshire, 1663-4', *C.Sf.* 3rd series **10**, 1914, 53, 55, 57, 60 & 63. Minshull family.

Molyneaux

See Latham

Monk

'The Monk family of Chester *C.Sf.* 3rd series **25**, 1931, 9. 18-19th c.

Mottrum

RENAUD, F. 'Mottrum of Mottrum, in the parish of Prestbury, *L.C.A.S.* **19**, 1901, 38-44. Medieval; includes pedigree.

Moulson

'Moulson *alias* Moulton', *C.Sf.* 3rd series **4**, 1902, 14-15. See also **5**, 1904, 105. 16-18th c.

Mynshull
See Minshull

Nelstrop
William Nelstrop & Co. Ltd., Stockport: 150 years 1820-1970. Stockport: Wm. Nelstrop & Co., 1970. Includes information on the Nelstrop family.

Neuton
'Entries in a folio Bishop's Bible ...', *M.G.H.* 2nd series **5**, 1894, 200. Neuton and Mere families, 16th c.

Nevil
PLANCHE, J.R. 'On the Norman ancestry of the Nevils, and the origin of the armorial bearings of the line of Raby', *Journal of the British Archaeological Association* **22**, 1866, 279-90.
See also Audeley

Nevitt
B[ENNETT], J.H.E. 'Family of Nevitt', *C.Sf.* 3rd series **21**, 1926, 54-95, *passim.* 16-19th c., includes wills.

Newton
McINNIS, JEAN. 'The story of a family', *F.H.S.C.J.* **20**(3), 1991, 5-15. Newton family of Birkenhead, 19th c.

Nield
TRUNKFIELD, ROGER. 'The Nields of Knutsford: the Balmoral connection', *Journal of the Knutsford Historical and Archaeological Association* **1**(4), 1979, 34-5. 17-19th c.

Norbury
HARRIMAN, G. 'The Norbury family of Marple: family bible entries', *N.C.F.H.* **13**(3), 1986, 90. 18-19th c.

Norris
B[ENNETT], J.H.E. 'The Norris family at Blacon Hall', *C.Sf.* 3rd series **39**, 1948, 12-13. 16-17th c.
See also Middleton

O'Brien
See Done

Offley
BOWER, G.C., & HARWOOD, H.W.F. 'Pedigree of Offley', *Genealogist* N.S., **19**, 1903, 217-31; **20**, 1904, 49-56, 78-86, 197-9 & 268-74. Of London, Staffordshire and Cheshire, 16-19th c.

Okill
BROWN, WM. E. 'The Okill family of the parish of Runcorn, and connections', *C.Sf.* 3rd series **22**, 1927, 70-71. 17-18th c.
W., T.L.O. 'The Okills of Grappenhall, Warrington and Liverpool', *C.Sf.* 3rd series **9**, 1913, 8-9 & 11-12. See also **12**, 1917, 33-4. 17-18th c.

Oliver
B[ENNETT], J.H.E. 'The Rev. Philip Oliver and his family', *C.Sf.* 3rd series **38**, 1948, 100-116, *passim* 17-18th c.

Ormesby
See Revesby

Orrell
CEDRIC. 'The Orrell family', *C.Sf.* 3rd series **14**, 1919, 3031. See also 35 & 50. 15-17th c.
F., H.B. 'The Orrell and Wilkinson families', *C.Sf.* 3rd series **19**, 1924, *passim.* 17-18th c.
F., H.B. 'The Orrell family', *C.Sf.* 3rd series **18**, 1923, 29-30. Includes extracts from Wilmslow registers, 1559-1626; also will of Thomas Orrell of Chorley, 1602.

Owen
'Family bible', *N.C.F.H.* **14**(4), 1987, 103. Entries relating to the Owen family of Wrenbury, 18-19th c.

Paris
'The Paris family of Chester', *C.Sf.* 3rd series **51**, 1956, 489. See also **52**, 1957, 6. 14th c.

Parker
SIMPSON, EILEEN. 'The Parkers, poverty, and Little Peover', *Cheshire history newsletter* **9**, 1975, 20-23. 18th c.

Parnell
COOPER, THOMAS. 'The Parnell family', *C.N.Q.* N.S., **1**, 1896, 118-23. See also 231-2. Includes pedigree 16-19th c.
See also Lancelyn

Perryn
HERFORD, A.F. 'The Perryn family of Cheshire', *C.Sf.* 3rd series **6**, 1907, 31 & 43. 18-19th c. 'The Perryn family of Flintshire and Chester', *C.Sf.* N.S., **1**, 1895, 98-9. See also 111-12. 18th c.

Pickering
B[ENNETT] J.H.E. 'Visitation of Cheshire, 1663-4: Pickering of Walford and Thellwall, Co. Chester', *C.Sf.* 3rd series **11**, 1915, 57. Reprinted from *M.G.H.* N.S., **4**, 1884, 405. 'Pedigree of the family of Fletcher: Pedigree B: Pickering and Keen', *M.G.H.* N.S., **4**, 1884, 232. 17-18th c.

Pierrepont
LEWIS, G.R. 'A Cheshire branch of the Pierrepont family', *N.C.F.H.* **6**(1), 1979, 20-21. 18th c.

Pigot
TWEMLOW, FRANCIS R. Pigot family, of Butley and Bonishall, Co. Chester, of Chetwynd, Co. Salop, and of Mere and Forton, Co. Stafford', *C.Sf.* 3rd series **16**, 1921, 55-60, *passim.* 15-16th c.

Pine
See Rowe

Plant
PLANT, W.K. 'Marriage extracts from the Plant family tree', *F.H.S.C.J.* **11**(3), 1982, 5-6; **11**(4), 1982, 13-14. Plant family marriages, 16-19th c.

Platt
CUMMINS, W.A. 'Was Ezra Platt a bigamist?', *F.H.S.C.J.* **3**(1) 1972, 8-10. Platt family, 18-19th c.

Pole
See Poole

Poole
H., T. 'Poole of Poole, Co. Chester, *C.Sf.* 3rd series **5**, 1904, 64-5. 14-16th c., *alias* Pole. Also of Shute, Devon.
POOLE, MARGARET ELLEN. 'The Poole family of Poole Hall in Wirral', *H.S.L.C.* **52**, N.S., **16**, 1900, 165-216. Medieval-19th c.

Stewart-Brown
STEWART-BROWN, R. 'Composition papers of Thomas Poole of Poole, Co. Chester, and other members of his family', *C.Sf.* 3rd series **9**, 1913, 47-8. Mid 17th c.

Pratchett
'Family of Pratchett of Worleston, Co. Chester', *C.Sf.* **56**, 1963, 28-37, *passim.* 16-18th c.

Prayers
W., A. 'Certificate by the Black Prince regarding Thomas de Prayers of Barthomley, Cheshire, dated 1343', *Archaeological journal* **14**, 1857, 349-52. Includes genealogical notes on Prayers family.

Proby
CRAWFORD, GIBBS PAYNE. 'The family of Proby in Chester and Ireland', *J.C.A.H.S.* N.S., **28**(1), 1928, 97-105. Includes pedigree, 17-19th c.

Pulford
See Revesby

Radmore
L., P.H. 'The Radmore and Brassey families', *C.Sf.* 3rd series **17**, 1922, 3. See also 8. 17-18th c.

Ravenscroft
EDWARDS, F.H. 'The family of Ravenscroft', *C.F.H.* **3**, 1974, 19-23. 16-19th c.
RAVENSCROFT, W., & RAVENSCROFT, R. BATHURST. *The family of Ravenscroft.* Mitchell Hughes and Clarke, 1915. Reprinted from *M.G.H.* Pedigrees. The family was originally of Cheshire, but subsequently of London and many other counties.

Ravenshaw
RAVENSHAW, JOHN. *A short account of the family of Ravenshaw of Ash, Richmond & Baddington; also of Renshaw de Orea, with a few Raynshaw wills.* Privately printed, 1908. Includes extracts from various records, with pedigrees, medieval-19th c. Also includes pedigrees of Withers and Hockenhull.

Raynshaw
See Ravenshaw

Renshaw

RENSHAW, WALTER CHARLES. *Collections relating to some Renshaws, particularly of Cheshire.* Chiswick Press, 1893. 16-19th c., includes folded pedigree, extracts from the parish register of Bowdon, lists of wills, *etc. See also* Ravenshaw

Revesby

SITWELL, SIR GEORGE. *The barons of Pulford in the eleventh and twelfth centuries and their descendants, the Revesbys of Thrybergh and Ashover, the Ormesbys of South Ormesby, and the Pulfords of Pulford Castle, being an historical account of the lost baronies of Pulford and Dodleston in Cheshire, of seven Knight's fees in Lincolnshire attached to them, and of many manors, townships and families in both counties.* Scarborough: Sir George Sitwell, 1889. Includes deed abstracts, medieval.

Robinson

L., P.H. 'Thomas Robinson of Chester, goldsmith', *C.Sf.* 3rd series **12**, 1917, 38. Extracts from family bible, early 18th c.

Roe

B[ENNETT], J.H.E. 'Roe family of Macclesfield and Liverpool', *C.Sf.* 3rd series **30**, 1935, 72-99. 17-19th c.
'Charles Roe of Macclesfield (1715-81): an eighteenth-century industrialist', in CHALONER, W.H. *Palatinate studies: chapters in the social and industrial history of Lancashire and Cheshire,* ed. W.R.Ward. Cm.S., 3rd series **36**, 1992, 51-101. Includes pedigree, 18-19th c.

Rogers

S., A.G. 'The parentage of Archdeacon Robert Rogers', *C.Sf.* 3rd series **29**, 1935, 10-11. 16th c.

Rowe

ROWE, J.Y. 'Some Rowe-Pine-Coffin connections', *Devon and Cornwall notes and queries* **30**(1), 1965, 15-18. Of Cheshire, Leicestershire and Devon; mainly medieval.

Rutter

HELSBY, T. 'Le Roter, or Rutter, of Kingsley, Co. Pal. Chester', *Reliquary* **12**, 1871-2, 129-38 & 229-38. 16-19th c.

Saint

See Sant

Saint-Saviour

See Statham

Salkeld

MOORE, J. GRANGE. *Salkelds through seven centuries.* Phillimore, 1988. Of Cumberland, Yorkshire, Suffolk, Shropshire and Cheshire., includes pedigrees, probate records, *etc.*

Sandbach

POOLE, BILL. 'The Sandbach family of Burton, Tarporley', *Lancashire and Cheshire historian* **1**, 1965, 173-4. 19th c.

Sant

SANT, A.J. 'The quest, part 4: into the past', *N.C.F.H.* **10**(4), 1983, 95-8. Sant or Saint family 17-19th c.

Savage

IVES, E.W. 'Crime, sanctuary, and royal authority under Henry VIII: the exemplary sufferings of the Savage family', in ARNOLD, M.S., *et al,* eds. *Of the laws and customs of England: essays in honour of Samuel E. Thorne.* Chapel Hill: University of North Carolina Press, 1981, 296-320.

Scragg

SCRAGG, JOAN R. 'The origins of the Scragg family in Cheshire', *F.H.S.C.J.* **11**(4), 1982, 10-11; **12**(1), 1982, 11-12. 18-20th c.

Shaw

RENSHAW, WALTER CHARLES. *Notes relating to some Shaws of Cheshire.* Chiswick Press, 1891.
SHAW, R. CUNLIFFE. 'Two fifteenth-century kinsmen: John Shaw of Dukinfield, mercer, and William Shaw of Heath Charnock, surgeon', *H.S.L.C.* **110**, 1958, 15-30.

Shelmerdine

Extracts from church register relating to the family of Shelmerdine. Mitchell and Hughes 1879. 17-19th c. Mainly from Northenden.

Shuttleworth

CONROY, MICHAEL P. *Backcloth to Gawthorpe.* Nelson: Hendon Publishing, 1971. Shuttleworth family, medieval-20th c.

Smith

B[ENNETT], J.H.E. 'The Smith family of Chester and Hough', *C.Sf.* 3rd series **32**, 1938, 65-6. 18th c.

HALL, JOHN R. 'A century of Smith family history, 1800-1900', *N.C.F.H.* **14**(2), 1987, 35-7; **14**(3), 1987, 69-71; **14**(4), 1987, 100-102. Of Longdendale.

RYLANDS, J. PAUL. 'An illuminated pedigree of the family of William Smith, Rouge Dragon Pursuivant of Arms, AD 1605', *Genealogist* **6**, 1882, 212-6. 15-16th c.

Smith-Carington

COPINGER, WALTER ARTHUR. *History and records of the Smith-Carington family from the Conquest to the present time, with full account of the various seats and places with which its members have been connected, including Carrington in Cheshire, Ashby Folville in Leicestershire, Wotten Wawen in Warwickshire and Blackmore and other places in Essex ...* H. Sotheran and Company, 1907. Extensive; includes numerous pedigrees, some folded in a separate wallet.

Spann

B[ENNETT], J.H.E. 'Spann family of Bromborough. *C.Sf.* 3rd series **40**, 1948, 11-81, *passim.* 16-18th c. Includes wills.

Spurstow

'Spurstow of Spurstow family', *C.Sf.* 3rd series **16**, 1921, 378. Medieval.

Stanier

See Stone

Stanley

CASH, SARAH. 'The Stanleys of Alderley', *C.N.Q.* **6**, 1901, 172-8. Medieval-19th c.

COWARD, B. 'A crisis of the aristocracy on the sixteenth and early seventeenth centuries? The case of the Stanleys, Earls of Derby, 1504-1642', *Northern history* **18**, 1982, 54-77.

EARWAKER, J.P. 'Extracts from the register of Eastham, Co. Chester: the Stanley family of Hooton', *C.Sf.* N.S., **1**, 1895, 88-9. 17th c.

IRVINE, W. FERGUSSON. 'The early Stanleys', *H.S.L.C.* **105**, 1953, 45-68. Includes folded pedigree, 12-15th c., and abstracts of 34 deeds.

LAWSON, PHILIP H. 'Family memoranda of the Stanleys of Alderley, 1590-1601 and 1621-1627', *J.C.A.H.S.* N.S., **24**(2), 1920-21, 81-101.

MITFORD, NANCY, ed. 'The ladies of Alderley, being the letters between Maria Josepha, Lady Stanley of Alderley, and her daughter in law, Henrietta Maria Stanley, during the years 1841-1850. Hamish Hamilton, 1967. Originally published 1938. Includes pedigree, 18-20th c.

MITFORD, NANCY, ed. *The Stanleys of Alderley: their letters between the years 1851-1865.* [New ed.] Hamish Hamilton, 1968.

WEAVER. 'The Stanleys of Alderley', *C.Sf.* **3**, 1891, 229-30. Brief notes.

WILSON, E. 'Sir Gawain and the green knight and the Stanley family of Stanley, Storeton and Hooton', *Review of English studies* **30**, 1979, 308-16. Includes brief 14th c. pedigree.

Starkey

DALE, A. 'Starkey records', *Lancashire and Cheshire historian* **1**, 1965, 79-80. See also 32. Extracts from Daresbury registers, 17th c.

STATHAM, S.P.H. *The descent of the family of Statham, containing an account of the Saint-Saviours, Viscounts of the Cotentin, the Barony of Malpas, Co. Chester, the Lymmes of Lymme, Co.Chester, the Bolds of Bold, Co. Lancaster, the Stathums of Stathum, Co. Chester, the Stathams of Morley, Co. Derby, and of Leicestershire, Australia and U.S. America.* Times Book Company, 1925. Medieval-20th c., includes folded pedigrees.

Steel

R[YLANDS], J.P. 'The visitation of Cheshire 1663-4: Steel of Coppenhall, Co. Chester', *C.Sf.* 3rd series **10**, 1914, 18-19. 17th c.

BODDINGTON, R.S. 'Extracts from the parish registers of Sandbach, Cheshire, relating to the Steele family', *M.G.H.* N.S., **2**, 1877, 384-5.

Stiles
B[ENNETT], J.H.E. 'The Stiles family of Chester', *C.Sf.* 3rd series **14**, 1919, 18-19. 16-17th c.

Stokeport
ORMEROD, GEORGE. *The early conversion of the Anglo-Norman families of Stokeport, Fitz-Roger, Banastre and Gernet.* [ ]: [ ], 1851.

Stonehewer
COOPER, THOMAS. 'Stonehewer-Stonyer-Stanier: an old Cheshire family settled at Barleyford, near Macclesfield', *C.N.Q.* N.S., **3**, 1898, 64-6. 16-17th c.

Stonyer
See Stonehewer

Strettell
B., E.L.W. 'The Strettells of Mobberley', *A.N.Q.* **4**, 1884, 66-7. Pedigree, 16-17th c.

Strettle
See Hulme

Stringer
B[ENNETT], J.H.E. 'The visitation of Cheshire, 1663-4: Stringer of Crewe', *C.Sf.* 3rd series **10**, 1914, 44-5.

Sutcliffe
'[Sutcliffe family bible entries, 1754-1814]', *F.H.S.C.J.* **8**(3), 1979, 22.

Swain
SWAIN, SYDNEY A. 'Annie's ancestors', *C.F.H.* **2**, 1974, 15-16 & 24; **4**, 1974, 19-20. See also **5**, 1975, 20-21, & **6**, 1975, 24-6. Swain family, 18-19th c.

Tarleton
S[TEWART]-B[ROWN], R. 'Tarleton of Bolesworth, Co. Chester', *C.Sf.* 3rd series **16**, 1921, 8. See also 15. 17th c.
STEWART-BROWN, R. 'Tarleton of Bolesworth Castle, Co. Chester', *C.Sf.* 3rd series **27**, 1934, 50-64, *passim.* 17-18th c.

Tatton
NICHOLSON, J. HOLME. 'The Tattons of Wythenshawe', *C.N.Q.* **6**, 1886, 199-200. Medieval-17th c.
'Cheshire families: Tatton of Withenshaw', *A.N.Q.* **1**, 1882, 153-5.

Thorpe
'A famous Cheshire family', *C.N.Q.* N.S., **8**, 1908-11, 57-62. Thorpe family, 18-19th c.

Tillesley
GATFIELD, GEORGE. 'A fifteenth century marriage contract', *Genealogist* N.S., **7**, 1891, 245-6. Marriage of John Tillesley amd Jane Mascy.

Touchet
'A vellum pedigree-roll of the family of Touchet, of Nether Whitley and Buglawton, Co. Chester, and Touchet, Baron Audley, of Heleigh, Co. Stafford', *Genealogist* N.S., **36**, 1920, 9-21. Medieval.

Townshend
A., H.I. 'Townshend', *Notes and queries* **165**, 1933, 322-3. See also 356-7. Of Chester and Christleton, 16-18th c.
FLETCHER, W.G.D. 'The family of Townshend of Chester and Christleton, &c', *C.Sf.* 3rd series **8**, 1911, 5-6. See also 456 & 63-4; **9** 1913, 79, 81 & 101. 17-18th c.

Trafford
RYLANDS, J. PAUL. 'Henry Trafford, vicar of Burton; Thomas Trafford, rector of Heswall and Pembridge; John Banner, vicar of Stoak, and Richard Banner, vicar of Stoak and Eastham',*C.Sf.* 3rd series **9**, 1913, 35-6, 37-9 & 40-41. 17th c.

Troutbeck
BROWNBILL, JOHN. 'The Troutbeck family', *J.C.A.H.S.* N.S., **28**(2), 1929, 147-79. Includes folded pedigree, 14-15th c.

Twanbrook
See Twenebroke

Twenebroke
RYLANDS, JOHN PAUL. *Twenebrokes or Twanbrook, of Appleton, Grappenhall and Daresbury, in the County of Chester, A.D 1170 to 1831.* Liverpool: Thomas Brakell, 1887.

RYLANDS, JOHN PAUL. 'Twenebrokes, or Twanbrook, of Appleton, Grappenhall and Daresbury in the County of Chester, A.D. 1170 to 1831', *H.S.L.C.* 37; N.S., 1, 1888, 1-20. See also 116. Includes pedigrees, 12-19th c., deed abstracts, wills, parish register extracts, *etc.*

Underhill

WRIGHT, J. 'The Underhill family of Macclesfield, 1790-1890', *N.C.F.H.* 5(3), 1978, 72-6.

Vanbrugh

HISTORICUS. 'Sir John Vanbrugh, architect and dramatist', *C.Sf.* 3rd series 5, 1904, 19. Includes extracts from the parish register of Holy Trinity, Chester, late 17th c.

Vawdrey

RENSHAW, ISRAEL J.E. 'The Vawdrey family of Riddings, parish of Bowdon', *P.N.* 1, 1881, 88-9. 17th c. extracts from a 'family register'.

Venables

BROWN, HENRIETTA BRADY. *Some Venables of England and America, and brief accounts of families into which certain Venables married.* Cincinnati: Kinderton Press, 1961. Medieval-20th c.

Walthall

'Walthall: Wistaston registers, Cheshire', *M.G.H.* 2nd series 2, 1888, 298-9. Extracts, 17-18th c.

Warburton

BAILEY, J.E. *The Warburtons of Arley.* Manchester: [ ], 1881. Reprinted from *Papers of the Manchester Literary Club* 7. 14-18th c.

BARLOW, T.W. 'Warburton of Warburton', *Cheshire and Lancashire historical collection* 2 1855, 17-22. 16-17th c.

NOTON, J. 'The Warburtons of Arley', *P.N.* 4, 1884, 216-9. Medieval.

R[YLANDS,] J.P. 'The Warburtons of Broomfield, within Appleton, Co. Chester', *Lancashire and Cheshire antiquarian notes* 2, 1886, 42-4. Parish register extracts *etc.*, 16-17th c.

WARBURTON, NORMAN. *Warburton: the village and the family.* Research Publishing, 1970. Warburton family, 16-20th c. Includes pedigree, will abstracts, list of Warburton parish officers, extracts from parochial accounts, *etc.*

Warren, Earls of

WATSON, JOHN. *Memoirs of the ancient Earls of Warren and Surrey and their descendants to the present time.* Warrington: William Eyres, 1782. v.2. includes the Warrens of Poynton and the barons of Stockport, 14-18th c.

Werden

HEWITT, JOHN. 'Werden family of Chester', *C.Sf.* 3rd series 8, 1911, 19-70. See also 55. 17-18th c.

HUGHES, T. 'The Werdens of Chester and Burton, *C.Sf.* 3, 1891, 43. 17th c.

Wharton

WHARTON, EDWARD ROSS. *The Whartons of Wharton Hall.* Oxford: Oxford University Press, 1898. 16-18th c.

Whishaw

WHISHAW, JAMES. *A history of the Whishaw family.* Methuen & Co., 1935. 16-20th c.

Whitaker

COLLINSON, H. 'An account of the family of Whitaker of Warwickshire and Lancashire, with their Cheshire connections', *N.C.F.H.* 6(4), 1979, 101-5, 7(1), 1980, 5-9. Medieval-19th c.

Whitley

PEMBERTON, L.M. 'Whitley family of Norley', *C.Sf.* 3rd series 22, 1927, 84-5. See also 88 & 90; 23, 1928, 1-2 & 6-7; 24, 1928, 78-9 & 84; 25, 1931, 3-12, *passim.* 17-19th c.

STEWART-BROWN, R. Whitley family of Aston Hall and elsewhere', *C.Sf.* 3rd series 25, 1931, 63-79, *passim.* 17-19th c., includes wills.

Whittell

W., H. 'Robert Whittell, M.A., rector of Tarporley, 1613 to 1638', *C.Sf.* 3rd series 25, 1931, 16-17 & 18-19. Includes pedigrees, 11-17th c.

S., A.G. 'Whittell or Whittle family of Chester, etc.', *C.Sf.* 3rd series **31**, 1937. 23. See also 73-4. Late 18th c.

W., H.M. 'The families of Whittell or Whittle of Chester', *C.Sf.* 3rd series **25**, 1931, 82-4 & 88; **26**, 1934, *passim.* 14-18th c.

Whittingham

B., J. Whittingham of Whittingham and Middlewich', *C.Sf.* 3rd series **24**, 1929, 55-6. 16th c.

'A pedigree of the Cheshire families of Whittingham and Berington, drawn on vellum and painted by the third Randle Holmes of Chester in 1664', *Genealogist* N.S., **30**, 1914, 145-9. Also of Lancashire.

Wilkinson
See Orrell

Williams

'John Williams, Sheriff of Chester, 1587', *C.Sf.* 3rd series **12**, 1917, 1-15, *passim.* Pedigree, medieval.

YARWOOD, NORAH. 'The William and Wright syndrome', *N.C.F.H.* **1**, 1972, 12-13. Includes Williams family tree, 19-20th c.

Withers
See Ravenshaw

Wright

G., A.D. 'The Wrights of Offerton and Mottram-St-Andrew', *C.N.Q.* **6**, 1886, 29-31. Pedigree, 17-19th c.

'Wright family of Brewers Hall, Chester', *C.Sf.* 3rd series **29**, 1935, 56.

See also Williams

Wyche

BROOKE, RICHARD. 'On the ancient family of Wyche, or De La Wyche, with a descriptive account of their seat at Alderley in Cheshire', *H.S.L.C.* **1** 1849, 11-17. 17-19th c.

WYCHE, C.H. DE LA. 'The Wyche family of Alderley', *C.Sf.* 3rd series **26**, 1934, 5-6. See also 17-18. 17-19th c. pedigree.

Yale

TOWNSHEND, CHAS, HERVEY. 'Pedigree of Yale', *New England historical and genealogical register* **53**, 1899, 82-3. 17th c.

Yates

RUNYON, ETHEL DALE. 'David Yates' family: Lancashire, Cheshire, and points beyond', *Manchester genealogist* **30**(3), 1994, 10-14. 18-19th c.

ARNOLD, HILARY. 'The Yates family of Smallwood', *F.H.S.C.J.* **18**(1), 1988, 13-18. 19th c.

Family Name Index

36

Place Name Index

39

Author Name Index

A., H. 32
Adams, A. 9
Angel, C. 19
Angus-Butterworth, L. 9
Antrobus, R. 14
Antrobus, S. 14
Armytage, G. 9
Arnold, H. 34
Arnold, M. 30
Axon, G. 14

B., E. 32
B., J. 24, 34
Bailey, J. 33
Barlow, J. 15
Barlow, T. 33
Beamont, W. 14, 21, 25
Beazley, F. 15, 18, 27
Beckett, F. 15
Bell-Jones, W. 16
Bennett, F. 23
Bennett, J. 11, 14-17, 20, 23-32
Bewley, E. 22
Bingley, R. 16
Birchenough, J. 16
Boddington, R. 32
Booth, J. 16
Boram, J. 26
Bostock, R. 16
Bowden, C. 16
Bower, G. 28
Bradford, W. 16
Braunsdorff, O. 26
Brentnall, J. 17
Bridgeman, C. 14
Brooke, R. 17, 34
Broughton, S. 20
Brown, H. 33
Brown, W. 28
Brownbill, J. 32
Buckler, J. 23
Bullock, C. 19
Bullock, M. 18

Carr, P. 23
Carter, W. 19

Cash, S. 20, 31
Cedric 28
Chaloner, W. 30
Chorlton, R. 21
Cole, A. 21
Collinson, H. 33
Conroy, M. 31
Cook, E. 26
Cook, N. 21
Cooper, K. 16
Cooper, T. 9, 28, 32
Copinger, W. 31
Cottingham, E. 19
Cotton, B. 26
Coward, B. 31
Crawford, G. 29
Crawford, P. 23
Cromwell, L. 20
Croston, J. 9
Crozier, M. 17
Cruickshank, D. 21
Cummins, W. 29

Dale, A. 14, 31
Davenport, A. 20
Davies-Colley, T. 19
Delamere, B. 20
Dod, O. 20
Dredge, J. 9
Drinkwater, C. 20
Driver, J. 26
Dwarris, F. 17
Dwarris, S. 17

E., H. 21
Eachus, F. 21
Earle, T. 21
Earwaker, J. 24, 31
Edwards, F. 29

F., H. 28
Falk, B. 17
Fergusson, R. 20
Figueiredo, P. 9
Finley, R. 27
Finney, S. 21
Fletcher, W. 20, 32

Fowler, G. 27
Fryer, W. 16

G., A. 34
Gaskell, E. 10
Gatfield, G. 32
Genealogist 18
Gibbon, E. 22
Glasgow, R. 23
Gleave, G. 14
Gleave, S. 22
Goldie, E. 23
Green, R. 25
Griffin, R. 10

H., J. 27
H., T. 15, 29
Hall, J. 24, 31
Hance, E. 15
Harriman, G. 28
Harwood, H. 28
Head, R. 10
Heape, C. 23
Heape, R. 23
Helsby, T. 23, 30
Herford, A. 29
Hewitt, J. 11, 12, 15, 17, 33
Heywood, P. 15
Hibbert, L. 16
Hibbert, T. 15
Highet, T. 20
Historicus 22, 33
Holland, E.S. 24
Holmes, R. 34
Holt, B. 24
Howard, J. 23
Hughes, R. 18
Hughes, T. 13, 14, 17, 33
Hulland, J. 23
Hulley, R. 24

Iredale, D. 27
Irvine, W. 9, 19, 24, 31
Ives, E. 30

Jones, M. 23
Jones, R. 20